KIRKLANDPARK PRIMARY SCHOOL

STRATHAVEN

Junior School Art

Junior School Art

Kenneth Jameson

Studio Vista London

Acknowledgements

The author and the publisher wish to thank the pupils and staff of schools in London and Croydon for providing illustrations and creative writing; The Society of Assistants Teaching in Preparatory Schools for permission to reproduce figs. 20, 47, 108c, 108d, and 112a; teacher-members of in-service Junior Art and Craft Courses for figs. 49, 76, 99a, 99b, 108a; Mrs P. C. Francis for help and co-operation with experimental teaching sessions; Mrs Mary Seyd for fig. 112b; Michael Grater Esq. for fig. 107; John Kenway Esq. for permission to quote passages from his writings, page 84; Francis Carr Esq. for permission to include figs. 83a and 83b; Ralph Brown Esq. for permission to include fig. 84; the Tate Gallery for figs. 6 and 61d; Kunsthaus, Zurich, for fig. 82; J. M. Dent Ltd for the quotation from *Under Milk Wood* by Dylan Thomas in page 83; Penguin Books Ltd, publishers of *Gerard Manley Hopkins, Prose and Verse*, for the quotation from *The Starlight Night* in page 83, Mrs E. Defferary for preparing the typescripts and, finally, Mrs Norma Jameson for many kinds of help and support during the preparation of text and illustrations for publication.

© Kenneth Jameson 1971

Reprinted 1973 and 1976

A Studio Vista book published by
Cassell & Collier Macmillan Publishers Ltd.
35 Red Lion Square. London WC1R 4SG
and at Sydney, Auckland, Toronto, Johannesburg,
an affiliate of
Macmillan Publishing Co. Inc.,
New York

Set in 11 pt Times (Lumitype)

Printed and bound in Great Britain by
Butler & Tanner Ltd, Frome and London

ISBN 0 289 70044 2

Contents

Introduction

Part 1

1   The intake 9
2   The dual role of art 10
3   Colour, paints 13
4   The elements of art 30
5   Drawing 48
6   Autumn Frieze 54
7   Integrative teaching 68
8   Creativity, originality, stimuli, change 77
9   Environment 90
10 Revolution and variation 97
11 The fine arts 102
12 The teacher 108

Part 2

Basic skills: 112
Composition 112
Printing 114
Clay 121
Carving 126
Puppetry 127
Fabric 129
Mosaic 133
Paper 135
Wood 137
Wire 138
Junk modelling 139
String 140
Conclusion 141
Further reading 142
Index 143

Comparative Grades

American readers should note that in the context of this book 'Junior' refers to children aged 7 to 11 years and is roughly equivalent to the Elementary grades, 6 to 12, in American Primary Schools.

U.S.		Britain	
0–5	No teaching before 5 'Headstart'; Nursery schools privately run	0–5	Playgroups, Nursery, Kindergarten
5–6	Kindergarten	5–7	Infant School
6–12	Elementary	7–11	Junior School
12–14	Junior High	11–18	Secondary School
14–18	High School	13–18	Secondary (Public) School
18+	College, University and Adult education	16/18+	College, University, Evening Institute, College of Further Education

Introduction

That part of education which takes place in schools, colleges, universities and evening institutes, is usually organised into five stages according to age. They are: first stage, birth to five years; second stage, five to seven years; third stage, from seven to eleven years; fourth stage, eleven to eighteen years; and, finally, eighteen years and beyond. These divisions hold good, with minor variations, in most countries.

Creative art in one form or another is, by design or accident, a component of education at all levels.

For the minority of children in the first stage responsibility for their education, art included, is shared between home, and either nursery school, kindergarten or playgroup. The others with no nursery school, kindergarten or playgroup to go to, must depend entirely on parents; and playgroups in England are concerned more with 'social integration' than with 'education' in the accepted sense of the word. Teaching as such is, or should be, excluded from their activities.

Regular schooling begins at 5 or 6 years of age and this second stage added to the first, defines that period in the child's life when he is at his most spontaneous and most fluent in the use of paint, drawing and modelling materials and so needs no formal art teaching. At this point in his development all he requires is that materials, space, equipment and encouragement should be available in a propitious situation.

Pupils taking art and craft at the fourth stage, that is at from 11 to 18 years, have the advantage of specially equipped studios, appropriate materials, and art-trained teachers. Those of the fifth stage, studying advanced vocational courses in colleges of art, university fine art departments, main courses in teacher training colleges, or advanced non-vocational courses in evening institutes, benefit in the same way from specialist equipment and help. In other words, the provision made for stages two, four and five is, in general, appropriate for the art needs of the pupils and students. So too, with reservations about some unpredictable factors (parental influences for instance*), is the provision for the first stage.

Stage three, the middle range of children of 7 to 11 years, on the other hand, is not well catered for in art and craft. By the age of 7 they have ceased to be 'spontaneous little children' and have become, or are in process of becoming, thinking boys and girls. They begin to need the same facilities as the secondary pupil receives; yet only rarely do they have art and

*See *Pre-School and Infant Art,* pp. 104 and 119, by Kenneth Jameson, Studio Vista, London; Viking Press Inc., New York.

craft studios or art-trained teachers. We will speak more of this later on.

In addition, stage three is subject to certain difficulties which are inherent in the system. Teachers are too frequently handicapped, through no fault of their own, by outmoded training, by in-growing practices, by lack of opportunity to develop their own artistic gifts. Those with a general training are compelled to teach art even though they have no inclination, experience, or aptitude to do so, and find themselves short of 'art' ideas.

Another inherent difficulty at stage three is that somewhere between the ages of 7 and 9 years children pass through a period of change. As stated above, they cease to be 'spontaneous little children'. Hitherto the symbol for a tree was enough. Now the boy, or girl, looks out at his environment and his symbol tree no longer satisfies him. At this stage the pupil wants to know how he can make it 'look right'. What must we do to help him to cross over from infancy to boyhood?

A third difficulty is the creeping paralysis caused by the growing misconception that to copy, for instance, a stage-coach from the encyclopaedia in the school library, or paint the sea round the papier-mâché model of an island, or make a poster for the school play, is a way of getting round the difficult business of teaching art; and that by this method geography, history, English/drama and art are 'integrated'. There is nothing wrong about making the pencil drawing of the stage-coach, about mixing the island's ultramarine powder-colour sea, about composing the lopsided Roman letters of the play poster. They may be good history, geography, English/drama but they have little or nothing to do with art. The difficulty we are considering here is a serious one and it springs from misconceptions about the functions of art in the curriculum at this stage of schooling. We can only overcome it by asserting that art at this level has a much more significant role to play than that of a servicing facility for other subjects. We need to find a way of making sure that art is used to the full, as an educational subject in its own right, with a unique contribution to make. In the absence of specialist art teachers for this range of children this is a tall order; but there are good omens. The system shows signs of changing; but until it does a way must be found to help both teachers and children to make good the deficiencies which exist at the moment.

A main aim of this book is to show that art can and should play a *dual* role in the education of the 7- to 11-year-old pupils, that on the one hand it *should* concern itself with stage-coaches, blue seas, and posters, theme and project, group activities; but, at the same time, and more importantly, that it must be used as an educational tool in its own right.

Part One

1 The intake

In Britain the state decrees that the child shall transfer from the infant school to the junior school at the age of 7 years. Administratively this is a tidy arrangement. Educationally it poses problems. Some 7-year-old children may have a mental age of 5, perhaps less. Others may be developmentally as far forward as an average 9-year-old. The teacher will be concerned with the child's developmental rather than with his chronological age. It is likely that the junior school will contain a mixture of late-developing infants (kindergarten children) and early-developing juniors. Some may still be at the spontaneous, symbol, stage in their art work and so will need little support. Others will have reached the self-critical, self-conscious stage when they will need considerable advice and help. The teacher's main problems at this stage are to discern just where the child stands, developmentally, and to devise differing approaches to teaching individual children in the same group, and also and specially to provide support for those pupils who have reached the second, self-critical, stage when it is no longer sufficient, as it was with the 5–7 age children, merely to set up the painting or craft situations and to leave the child to explore them.

A first step to solving these problems is to realize that the junior pupil has tried the painting and craft before, when he was an 'infant' (5–7 years), and he is now ready to move forward. In future the learning situations set up for him must call for something more than, for instance, the exploration of paint as paint; they must differ in kind. They should face the child with a challenge in the form of the need to solve art problems. The vital opportunity for exploration and discovery, which is the 'educational' factor, must remain but now must consist not so much in the sensual pleasure of what happens when the child dips a brush in the paint and pushes it against the paper, as in his discovery of his own personal and individual way of solving the painting problem.

He needs new opportunities for exploration and discovery through *thinking*, in addition to seeing and feeling. In the context of the problem-solving situation, in terms of art, he will find new and different experiences.

Many problem-solving situations will arise out of the learning of basic skills and these will be dealt with later in the book.

2 The dual role of art

The argument of this book is based upon the thesis that art can and should play two roles. The first and more important is the role of educator in its own right. The second is that of art taking its place, and playing its part, as one of the disciplines, in combined educational activities which may have any subject, including art, as the core subject.

The second of the two concepts above is widely accepted and practised, in Britain at any rate. The first is more important educationally and yet is less well understood. It must be understood if we are to provide situations for the children in which they will find, for themselves, meaningful personal, aesthetic and educational experiences; so let us begin by asking ourselves two basic questions.

The first is:
What do we mean by 'using art as an educational tool'?

And the second:
What are those special aspects of art which provide experiences which *only* art *can* provide?

Art and crafts as an educational tool

The arts and crafts contribute educationally to the development of the child by making him 'aware', by stimulating his imagination, by sharpening his senses and by providing him with forms of expression for his ideas and emotions. In the area of colour for instance he learns that red is something more than a viscous liquid in a glass jar, or a heap of powder in a mixing palette; that it is more than just a colour for painting the fire-engine he has made. By experimenting with mixing red he finds there are literally hundreds of reds; that the reds *he* mixes are different from the reds his classmates mix; that he likes some reds more than others. If enough red objects are imported into the classroom, and if these are deployed with the reds he and his friends have produced, he discovers he has the power to change the classroom environment, in which he spends so much of his time, that he can make it *glow* with red. When he has reached this stage it is likely he will want, or he may be persuaded, to experiment with blue, yellow, green, purple, and the rest. This exposure to colour in mass provides a visual experience which is unique to the art medium. If exposure is practised over a wide range of colours separately it is likely to result in the development of sensitivity to colour and of discrimination in the appreciation of colour. If we accept that colour is a vital component of our daily life then such development can be seen to be educational in essence. The teacher who devises ways of achieving such exposure can be said to be using colour (one of the elements of art) as an educational tool.

Texture, tone, pattern, line, are all suceptible to the same treatment, and provide similar avenues for exploration, discovery, and significant experience. This theme is developed at greater length in the next section.

The child's natural curiosity and acquisitiveness provide the teacher with the opportunity to involve him visually, and in a tactile way, with his natural and man-made environment.

Art, as a group-activity, gives a sense of security and social integration.

The pupil who gets to grips with the problems of making a pot, or a print, or a plaster carving will have a deeper understanding of the art of the potter, the print-maker, the sculptor, and he is likely to develop discrimination in these areas of experience.

Practice in the crafts develops physical co-ordination and provides that special satisfaction associated with the mastery of tools and technique. It gives experience of the nature of materials, and of the peculiar characteristics of clay, wood, metal, plastics and the rest. It provides the less academically minded pupil with an opportunity to taste success. The teacher will provide those media which in his judgement will most nearly meet the needs of the child and will help to round off his development as a person.

Study of works of art in the original or in reproduction, examination and preferably handling of examples of fine design related to discussion of the place of picture or design in its contemporary setting, or in the life of the past, will complement the pupil's knowledge of history and of the social scene.

The above are some of the experiences which I suggest are educationally valid and are essential to the all-round development of the pupil. They are all rooted in aesthetics. They constitute a good part of the case for art and crafts as a subject in their own right; of the use of art for educational ends.

We have to admit that it is one thing to use art in this way. It is another, more difficult, thing to judge the effectiveness of such use.

It is comparatively easy to assess the junior child's painting as *art*. It is more difficult to assess the significance to the child of that same work as education, or the value to the child of the experiences he gained while he was producing the work.

Unlike the situation in the infant's school the provision of paints, paper, easels, brushes, etc. is not by itself sufficient to ensure that painting will contribute significantly to the personal development of the junior school child.

Painting is one of the basic art skills which can be taught, and which should be learned by all schoolchildren. Against this it should be remembered that it is possible for a child to practise painting as part of the curriculum, throughout his school career, and yet to leave school having learnt little or nothing about, for instance, colour. It may be better to 'teach' colour than to teach painting; i.e. it may be more valuable, educationally, to think in terms of structuring situations which will involve the pupils in considerations of colour rather than exclusively in making pictures.

It is not until the basic skill of painting is purposefully used by the teacher to provide the children with access to activities of greater significance than the mere mechanical application of paint, that painting can be said to assume the role of a tool to provide experiences which result in educational benefit for the child who has reached the self-critical stage. Too frequently painting, at the 8–11-year level, degenerates into a meaningless splashing about with paint, with the children not knowing what they are doing, a situation which rapidly deteriorates into apathy, boredom and frustration: it is a situation which arises frequently as a result of 'Here is a list of subjects on the blackboard—you can do which one you like best.'

Let us return for a moment to the 'red' theme. As an experiment try the children with a simple problem-solving exercise. Provide all those taking part with a large sheet of paper and invite each child to mix as many different reds as they can find by trial and error and then paint them, in patches, side by side, on their paper until the surface is totally covered and no bare paper can be seen. This modest challenge seems always to capture their interest and enthusiasm. In order to solve the problem they are involved in experiences with valuable results, viz, appreciation of red, discrimination about red, personal choice of red, development of sensitivity to red, with likely transfer of this sensitivity to other colours. Every child can do this simple exercise in problem-solving. It is hardly possible to fail at it and nothing succeeds like success. Every child must experience success. Success breeds confidence, the kind of confidence which comes from the feeling of having won one's place among one's peers.

In the above experiment the emphasis has moved from the practical activity of applying paint to paper to the aesthetic experience of being visually, intellectually and emotionally involved with colour. Is it more important to 'teach' colour than to teach painting to the junior child?

The act of painting, by itself, can become mechanical, repetitive and meaningless; and the 'list of titles on the blackboard' does nothing to help this situation. For it to become significant, painting must be a means to an end; that of confronting the junior child with a situation calling for aesthetic problem-solving at a modest level. In the process it is likely he will find pleasurable involvement and in addition he will be called upon to think, to form judgements and make decisions. The practical activity is likely to remain much the same on any and every occasion, when the child engages in painting. The aesthetic experience will vary in intensity and kind. At one time he may find a new awakening of perception, may discover a new range of colours, a new adventure in seeing, a new development of likes and dislikes.

The power of art as an educational tool consists not so much in drawing, and painting and the other art activities, as in the aesthetic experiences provided by the basic elements of art, i.e. colour, line, pattern, tone, texture, shape, form; and the use of drawing, painting, collage, print-making, and the other forms, to explore these elements more deeply and by so doing, to develop in the pupils an awareness of the qualities of the elements.

3 Colour, paints

As we have started by using colour as an example let us continue with it a little longer. We accept that colour is a valid field for educational activity for the pupil. We must then look at ways of exploiting the educational potential of colour.

It is the job of the school to prepare pupils for life. Colour is one of the universal components of living. All the time and inescapably we are compelled to make decisions about colour, before we buy a new car, a dress, or decorate our house for instance. The development of a sense of colour is of value to us as individuals and also in the total social context.

A sense of colour *may* accrue if the child is left to himself to paint clowns, and galleons, and crinoline ladies and bonfire night, but, in a teacher-structured situation, with colour as the aim, a sense of colour may be inculcated more certainly, more positively and more quickly.

It will be apparent that if colour is our objective then we are no longer confined only to painting. Collage, embroidery, mosaic, appliqué, print-making, dyeing, coloured light, transparencies, colour projections, all can be included in the classroom activity.

Let us take a look at one example of these, collage. There is not much of educational value in merely sticking bits of paper on to another sheet of paper, or bits of any sort of material on to any background; but, if we stay within the context of colour, there may be much of educational value if a simple aesthetic problem is set, such as providing two or three coloured magazines, and suggesting to the pupil that he search through and cut, or tear, out all the blues which interest him and then make a collage with only blues arranged in a way which pleases him (fig. 7a).

What are the educational values? 'Appreciation of blue', 'discrimination about blue', 'development of sensitivity to blue', 'sensitivity to one aspect of colour' and so probably by transfer to 'sensitivity' to other colours and perhaps ultimately to colour in general.

The corollary of this is that the 'basic skill' of collage, by itself, does not get us very far educationally, but if this skill is used to involve the child in a form of aesthetic problem-solving, however modest (colour discrimination in this case), it becomes educationally significant. The teacher sets the aesthetic problem. This is a teacher-structured situation designed to bring about a pre-ordained educational result, i.e. development of sensitivity to colour.

Exercises such as the above may call for modification in class management. From time to time it may be a good thing to gather the class together to discuss or propound a central idea, such as the colour examples already outlined, and then let the pupils separate and try out in their own way what they have absorbed from what was said in discussion.

To recapitulate—

So far we have considered some of the educational values which can be drawn from colour by using two basic art skills, painting and collage, and by involving the pupils in colour problem-solving. The other basic media can be used similarly.

It is not only the different *media* which can be used for involving the pupils with colour. There are many other approaches to that problem all of which, in their own special way, will reinforce the power and meaningfulness of colour experiences. Let us consider some of them.

Colour games

Herbert Read stresses the value of play to the child and his development. Experience supports the idea that individual play and organized play in the form of games provides a fertile context for rich experiences, many of which are directly educational. Games generate enthusiasm, healthy competition, mental alertness and much more besides. Football promotes physical and visual co-ordination, and a sense of pattern and direction, amongst other values. Intellectual games like crosswords develop vocabulary. Charades bring out a sense of drama and acting ability, musical games utilize a sense of rhythm. Word games like Lexicon (U.S. spelling bee) test spelling; card games test and develop memory, chess calls for precognition and a sense of geometry. ·

If learning is couched in play activity it adds a new ingredient to the educational process, a new stimulus to the pupil to learn, the inducement of pleasure.

Some typical art-learning games are detailed below.

Colour memory game

Suppose you have a class of thirty-six 10-year-old boys and girls. Try the following with them.

Give each a strip of heavy white drawing paper 12×4 in. Invite each child to mix a colour with powder paint and paint it all over the 12×4 in strip. When dry cut each strip into two equal-sized strips 6×4 in. Let each child in the class take a different number between 1 and 36. Let him then write his number on the back of each of his two 6×4 in strips. Each child now has two 6×4 in strips of the same colour with the same number on the back. Teacher, or monitor, next collects one strip of 6×4 in from each child, takes them out into the corridor or the assembly hall and arranges the coloured strips in a long line on the floor, or on a long table or bench or pinned to a display board. The same is done by the children in the classroom.

The game is now ready to be played. The first child selects any coloured strip except his own which takes his fancy in the classroom, looks on the back. Perhaps the number is fourteen. He studies the colour carefully and then replaces the strip. The game is to carry a mental picture of the colour in his mind, and also the number, and to go out into the corridor, or wherever the other set of colours is, and, without looking at the number on the back, to identify by mental colour memory the 'pair' of the colour he chose in the classroom. When he has decided which he thinks is his 'pair' he turns the strip over. If the number on the back is the same as the number on the back of his choice in the classroom he scores. The percentage of·

accurate assessments made by each individual child may be highly reveal-
ing to the teacher.

The game can be made very exciting if the class is divided into two
teams.

Children enjoy this game which is, of course, much more than a game.
It develops and improves colour perception and increases sensitivity to
colour. It may also detect unsuspected cases of colour-blindness.

Play the game first using different colours. Then next, as a refinement.
paint the strips with variations of *one colour only*; i.e. all different shades,
and tones of blue, or red, or green. To be able to identify a particular yellow
out of thirty-six yellows would be a considerable feat! The second, refined
variation of the game poses two sets of problems, (1) that of mixing the
colours in the first place: and (2) subsequently of identifying the pairs by
the exercise of colour memory.

Colour matching game

The very young child below 5 years enjoys using bright strong colour. He
likes to use it neat. When he mixes he is only concerned to see what
happens when two or perhaps three colours are mixed together. It is a sort
of magic. Later, he will want to mix colours so as to produce a particular
colour which he wants to use for a special purpose. The ability to mix paints
together in order to arrive at a predetermined colour is one of the basic
skills of art which can be taught and which will be needed by the pupil of
9, 10 and 11 years. Every adult amateur will be aware of the difficulty of
mastering colour mixing in the early stages of learning to paint. Children
are likely to find the same, or perhaps even greater, difficulty.

If you look around you now as you read and note how many pure
colours—i.e. red, orange, yellow, green, blue, violet—there are in your
immediate vicinity, you will find there are not very many. There may be a
book with a bright jacket, a dress perhaps, a carpet, a fruit or a flower. But
look at the floor, the wall, the armchair, the road surface, the fence, father's
jacket. Very few of these are pure colours, i.e. the colours of the spectrum.

On this point one might talk with the 9-, 10- and 11-year-old children
about the spectrum, and the rainbow, and ask one's science colleague to
set up the light experiment using a thin beam of white light directed through
a prism to show how light breaks up into its component colours. A whole
lesson devoted to this would be well spent, and would open links with
science (light) and with geography (rainbow). The total dependance of
colour upon light could be discussed.

To return to the wall, armchair, road, fence; if these are not pure spectrum colours what sort of colours are they? A few leading questions will
soon elicit from the children the fact that the colours are duller, or dimmer,
or greyer. A navy blue jacket is in fact a dark dull blue. A khaki tunic is
a medium greyish yellow green. The problem is how to mix these colours.
The basic skill can be taught as follows. Provide black and white powder
paint, brush, water and paper. Ask the pupil to mix a patch of the darkest
grey he can make and place it on one side of the paper.

fig. 1   Tone scale

Next let him mix a patch of the lightest grey, and place it on the opposite side. Equidistant from these two let him place a square of grey exactly half-way, in tone, between. Next mix a medium dark grey and a medium light grey and place them in their appropriate place; see diagram, fig 1.

Now let us consider, analytically, the navy blue. Is it a pure spectrum colour? No. Is it a bright, or a dull, colour? Dull. Is it a light or a dark colour? It is dark. Compared with the five greys, which is it nearest to, in 'dark'ness? The very dark. If you mixed some very dark grey what colour would you need to add to it to make it into navy blue? . . . bright blue?

The khaki is medium grey plus dull greenish yellow. The red wood floor is medium dark grey plus dull red (burnt sienna).

The game can now begin. Make a list of objects whose colours are in-determinate and subtle: Jane's hair; teacher's jacket; Peter's school satchel (bag); the pavement (sidewalk); the school desks; the outside wall of the school; . . . the colour of the soil in the garden . . . packing case . . . sacking . . . brown-paper parcel . . . chair . . . Write each one on a slip of paper. Put them into a box and mix them round. Each pupil then takes a slip, reads what it says and then proceeds to match the colour of the object he has picked and paints a small patch of the 'colour-match' on his paper. He then returns the slip of paper to the box and takes another, repeating this until he has a collection of colour-matchings. This game will be seen to be self-motivating and self-pacing. Once the basic colour-mixing skill is acquired, it can be practised as an open-ended activity. The child with ini-tiative will soon dispense with the slips of paper and teacher's titles and will make his own choice of objects to colour-match. The exercise develops sen-sitivity to colour and gives the pupil greater control over colour when he is working on imaginative paintings.

A point to remember is that powder colour dries paler than when it is applied wet.

Colour identification game

The word 'red' conjures up a mental picture of red in general; crimson, or scarlet, light or dark, and many other variants. Sometimes one needs to identify a colour more exactly. One way which is frequently used is to link the name of a common object with the colour; lemon yellow, sky blue. In the case of 'red' for instance, if one needed to verbally identify a particular red, one might say 'it's a dullish scarlet with a tinge of brown in it'; but it would be quicker and more positive to say 'it's Ketchup red'. Ketchup red would conjure up a colour concept of an exact kind. Beetroot red would evoke a different red concept.

This game can be played in two ways:

(1) The teacher can offer a 'draw from a hat' of slips of paper each one bearing a description such as scrambled egg yellow; ice-cream pink; grass green; mud colour; weak tea colour; black coffee colour; cow colour (let them sort that one out!); smoke blue; Sheila's sweater colour; flour white; rust; carrots; raspberry colour. The children then mix the colour. Alternatively a list could be written large on the blackboard.

(2) A second version of the game is to ask the children to mix colours and paint them on, say, 8×10 in papers. These are then pinned up where all can see, and the children in turn are invited to call out a verbal equivalent of any colour which attracts them. Children display remarkable inventiveness in this.

The educational value of this exercise, again is to sharpen and focus the child's attention and reaction to colour . . . and to challenge him to an inventive, imaginative and creative use of words.

Playing with projection of colour

Most schools have projectors capable of showing 35-mm slides, and these can be used to play a part in providing new and exciting colour experiences for the children. This is the age of plastics, and amongst these is a wide assortment of transparent coloured plastics of varying thicknesses, available in rolls or sheets of all sizes. Many brands of commercial plastics are available in Britain and there are equivalents in America. In addition many consumer products are wrapped in coloured cellophanes, like candies, perfumes, cosmetics, dyes, and these can be salvaged and used.

Many teachers are photographers and they will very likely have an accumulation of plastic slide frames salvaged from redundant colour transparencies. If you can accumulate enough, give every child in the class one each. Also give out thin stiff card, Sellotape (U.S. Scotch tape) (1 in or 2 in width), strong adhesive and scissors.

If there are not enough professional plastic slide frames those available can be used as templates and a pencil can be run round the outside and inside edges to provide an outline of the required size. The card can then be cut to provide home-made card slide frames (see illustration over). Assemble a quantity of new transparent coloured plastic sheeting, and coloured cellophane wrappings and let the children use these to provide home-made colour slides. The method is to stick Sellotape over one face of the slide frame, then to stick an area of transparent colour on the sticky face of the Sellotape. Make sure it is pressed flat. Put it in the projector and observe the projected colour. Now encourage the children to experiment by adding other colours over the top of the first and project again. Encourage them to observe the effect of overlaying one colour with another, blue with yellow for instance, or blue with red. Build up your home-made slide by superimposing many colours by the simple device of sticking a layer of transparent Sellotape in between each layer of colour. When projected the accidental effects are often surprising and beautiful.

fig. 2   Slides

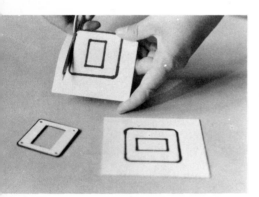

fig. 3   Tops

fig. 4   Whirling discs on string axis

This game calls for delicate manipulation of tools. It provides great excitement if every member of the class makes a slide and the teacher collects them all and organizes a ceremonial showing of the finished products. I have seen children hopping with impatience while waiting for their own particular slide to appear on the screen.

It is hardly possible to over-stress the importance of this kind of excited participation, or the value of thus focusing their looking.

Optical mixing of colour

The tops illustrated above were very simply made from stiff white cardboard (fashion board). A hole was pierced in the centre of each circular disc, a pointed piece of dowel rod slightly wider in diameter than the hole was forced through and a squeeze of strong adhesive was laid on the under side to join dowel to disc. Colours were painted on the discs and when the tops were spun, the colours merged; they mixed optically. One recalls whip-and-top games of years ago when children made chalk lines and rings on their wooden tops to achieve the same sort of visual result. A circular disc painted with, say, three segments of yellow and three of blue, equally spaced, shows green when spun. Blobs of colour give different results from stripes. The way two colours react together is different from the way three colours react. This simple device (fig. 4) provides many permutations. Children enjoy, and will spend much time, experimenting. This idea and much more besides is beautifully illustrated in *Seeing Colour*, a film for schools made by Margaret McEwan and distributed with other interesting 'colour' material by World Wide Pictures Ltd, 34 Cursitor Street, London, E.C.4. and U.S. Educational Teaching Aids, 159 West Kinzie St., Chicago, Illinois 60610.

Mechanically minded boys will find the optical mixing spinning-top principle can be convincingly demonstrated by using a small electric motor and by attaching the disc to the driving spindle; or alternatively by using a crank handle and gears and a construction set, such as Meccano.

Colour and the environment

Colour is so much part of daily life that we are constantly compelled to take it into account, to make judgements on it and decisions about it. We say that we like certain colours, that some colours suit us, it is the colours of the sunset which enthrall us. But how sure of ourselves are we? Let us suppose we have decided to buy a new car. We have decided the make and the model. We see four in the catalogue or the showroom, all in different colours. We choose, and it is a fairly simple choice to make. But suppose we are changing houses and the decorator asks us what colours we want for the interior. Are we as certain in this case? Can we choose colours and be sure they will 'look right' when they are on the walls, ceilings and doors? A good many people are so unsure of themselves in this matter that they are prepared to pay high fees to somebody else to make the decisions for them; and interior design consultants make a good thing out of it.

In the case of the car, the designer has solved the problem of colour for us. All we have to do is to make a straight choice of a completed article. In the case of the house we have to make a somewhat intimidating creative leap in the dark. We have to project our mind forward in time and try to assess what will be appropriate and aesthetically pleasing in our house interior. If our colour sense has been trained we shall be the better able to deal with such problems.

The colour 'games' already discussed are all directed towards the training of the colour sense. Another, aimed more specifically at developing a sense of the effect of colour upon the classroom environment, is an extension of the 'reds' example discussed previously, except that this time we will use yellows. Arrange for each pupil to have a large sheet of white paper, powder colours, brushes and water. Invite them to mix as many different yellows as possible and to cover their papers with patches of yellow arranged in such a way that they join, and no white paper shows through. Clear the largest display board in the classroom and when the 'yellows' are dry fasten them up, on the display board. A staple gun is a useful tool for doing this. Let each slightly overlap its neighbour so that the whole of the large display board is completely covered. Many education authorities provide large display boards, in the order of 25 × 4 ft, in classrooms. This provides space for a large area of yellow. The effect upon the environment of the classroom of a blaze of yellow such as we have been discussing above is prodigious. The children will respond to it. More than that, the

fig. 5 Staple gun

residual memory effect of the visual experience will remain. The impact upon daily life in the classroom will be invigorating, and will persist as long as the 'yellows' are left in position.

The educational effects of this project are the same as in previous games and exercises, but they are worth reiterating. They are:

> to encourage study of colour in depth, to develop colour discrimination and sensitivity, to make plain that there are infinite varieties even within one colour, and to provide practical experience of how colour can be made to play a positive part in the daily environment.

At the same time it might be wise to state that it is not the intention of this book to advocate games as the main approach in junior school art. Too much use of any one method will bore the children. The teacher knowing her own class will gauge how long any game should last. Some are more suitable for 'short bursts' with intervals of days between. Others may merit the spending of more time on each occasion. Remember the game is only of value if it is used as a means to achieve an educational end.

Ask all the children wearing blue sweaters or pullovers to stand up . . . to stand in a group . . . compare the different blues.

If the classroom provides the possibility of hanging strings across the room at ceiling height . . . try the device of making strings of triangular bunting, paint them all blue on one side and all green on the other. Make enough strings of bunting to saturate the room. The effect will be that from one end of the room there will be an overwhelming effect of green, and from the other end of blue. This is another variation on mixing as many versions of a single colour as the inventiveness of the pupils will permit. The effect of the exercise is to provide a visual colour bombardment upon the eyes of the pupils; to show them the power of colour to change their environment.

The teacher will be able to devise many more colour activities of a similar kind.

Colour, atmosphere, emotion

Children at the top end of the junior school are temperamentally ready to grapple with maturer concepts. The emotional or atmospheric use of colour is one such concept. It links strongly with the previous paragraph. If the classroom were draped with black and hung with masses of black bunting the pupils would be quick to identify the ominous mood created. Equally, a dazzling display of reds would evoke excitement. It is a short step from recognition of the fact that colour, of itself, can establish a mood, funereal or festive, to understanding Picasso's use of sombre blues, during his 'blue period', to overlay with a spirit of despair his paintings of the downtrodden working classes in Paris amongst whom as a poor man he lived at the turn of the century. Ten minutes or so spent in discussion with the children in front of any of Picasso's blue period pictures, his *Femme a la Chemise*, for instance, may plant a seed of new understanding of colour which may enrich their own subject paintings in due course (fig. 7b).

Colour can be used to strengthen the emotional content of a painting. In addition different colours can be used *together* to provide positive effects. For instance, a battle picture is more violent if clashing colours are used. A calm picture would be helped by harmoniously blending colours. A winter picture calls for cold colours; a jungle picture for hot colours. The children are quite capable of identifying the character of colours. They readily appreciate what is meant by hot colour, cold colour, harmonious colour, dissonant colour, red-hot, blue with cold, and so on.

At this point it must be firmly stated that there is no intention to decry or discourage familiar and long-established methods of picture-making. Very many children in the 9–11 age range get great satisfaction and pleasure from graphic work of that kind. Amongst other things it frequently leads to significant learning about colour. At the same time, as has been said, almost as frequently it can become a mindless activity. The danger is particularly great if the pupil is expected to produce pictures containing subject matter for which he has insufficient technique, or of which he has no direct personal experience. On the other hand the child's natural love of being able to produce a picture recognizable in content can be harnessed to, for instance, the study in depth of colour which we have been considering so far. This can be achieved by presenting the pupils with direct visual stimulus. Take an example. Spread a white cloth on a table and place it against a white wall. Place on the table a white plate, a bottle of milk, a white egg, a white basin, white flowers, a white jug and any other white object which may be to hand. Children who have been confronted by this stimulus register delight and surprise on seeing the exquisite and subtle differences of white. Emphasize that the *whites* are what matter if they attempt to interpret the subject in paint, and stress they need not include all the objects on display if they do not wish to. This exercise becomes a study, in depth, of white and takes its place as part of the wider study of colour generally.

Another example: imagine a boy dressed up in a red paisley dressing gown, a red scarf on his head tied as a turban. A red 'jewel' glitters in the front of it. He sits on a red mat in front of a screen hung with red material. In his hands he holds a red whistle, before him a red vase containing a red snake made from a lady's old nylon stocking. Behind the screen is a boy with rod and line. The snake-charmer plays upon his pipe, and the boy behind the screen slowly raises the rod, and the line which is attached to the snake. The snake is charmed out of the pot by the 'music'.

I was present when this drama was presented. It was a well-stocked classroom and all the props were available. The whole subject took very few minutes to prepare. The effect was exciting and entertaining. The boys aged 11 were presented with a dramatic visual image and they produced some fascinating paintings.

One is reproduced here (fig. 8). Once again this was an extension of the study in depth of colour, red. It was not presented as such but this was the structured situation. This was a purposeful use of picture-making to achieve a preconceived educational end, i.e. colour awareness.

Suppose the teacher had written 'snake-charmer' on the board and left it at that. Would the educational value have been so great? Would the children have been as stimulated? The subject was brought to life by this modest bit of dressing up.

Colour and science

There are innumerable interesting links between colour and other subjects. We have already referred to colour and the spectrum and suggested that the scientific light experiment of breaking up a beam of white light into the spectrum range could be carried out in the art lesson. And that the teacher might use the geography lesson time to consider the rainbow in the art context. Science time might similarly be used to consider the relationship of colours one to another, perhaps constructing a colour circle, the colour circle's proper place being in the field of science and optics. A slight shift will turn the pupil's attention from light, and light colours, to focus upon the sort of colours used by the artist, and by children in the art class at school. Where do the colours come from, how are they made; when is a colour a colour? When is a colour a pigment? It comes as a revelation to some people, and not only to junior pupils, to discover that pigments are manufactured from a wide range of materials both organic and mineral. Lapis lazuli, iron oxide, strontium, lead, peach stones, burnt bones, earth, coal tar, mercury, insects' wings, sulphur. This magical-sounding list could lead pupils to explore the intriguing subject of making their own colours. Iron oxide can be scraped, in the form of rust, from any decomposing iron surface. Carbon can be collected from any bonfire or fire grate. Log-wood chips provide red dye when steeped in water. Onion skins provide yellow, beetroot provides brown. The links between art, science, and natural history are obvious. It must not be thought however that the raw materials, just as they are, will produce paints. They need to be ground fine with a muller and a glass slab. A large pestle and mortar might grind the softer materials. The fine particles are then mixed with either gum (for water colour) or oil for oil colours; but even if the exact equipment is not available, usable paints can be made from local raw materials.

For the teacher who would like to explore the chemistry of colour further with the children there are inexpensive books which help. They are:

Simple Rules for Painting in Oils by A. P. Laurie, M.A., D.Sc. Winsor & Newton Ltd, Wealdstone, Harrow, Middx.

The Composition and Permanence of Artists Colours, Painting Media, Oils and Varnishes. Free on request from Winsor & Newton Ltd.

Both these books are available in the U.S. from Winsor & Newton Inc., 555, Winsor Drive, Secaucus, New Jersey 07094.

The Use of Vegetable Dyes by V. Thurston. Dryad Handicrafts Ltd, North Gates, Leicester, LE1 4QR.

Notice we have made no mention of colour theories. Colour is a visual subject. It helps to know that there are three primary colours, and three secondary colours; that the primaries are red, yellow and blue, and that these three cannot be obtained by any mixture of any other pigments, that the three secondaries are green, orange and purple, and that these *can* be obtained by mixing the appropriate pair of primaries; but this is the only rule of thumb which the child need know. The rest he can find by exploration and experiment and with advice from the teacher, if he asks for it.

Some practical considerations

Paints

For several decades now powder colours have remained the most popular type of paint in primary and secondary schools. It is probably true to say that there has never been, and there is not now, an ideal solution to the problem of which paints to supply to schools, but at least there are a number of alternatives. They are:

Powder colour
The usual method for use is by flat nine-hole plastic or metal trays to hold the dry powder colours. Mixing is carried out in separate smaller mixing palettes. The method is inclined to be wasteful and untidy in use and storage.

Powder colours are supplied in small, medium, large and very large tins.

Solid tempera blocks
Convenient. Usually used in trays of six or nine. It is sometimes necessary to scrub hard to get a rich paint film. It is not so easy to build up a thickness of paint, though it helps if blocks are freely moistened before use. Tidy in use and in storage.

PVA/acrylic paints
These are the newest addition to the range of school paints. They are water-based and are very quick drying. They are somewhat expensive and, junior/elementary pupils being what they are, are somewhat uneconomical. Even short exposure to the air, because of their quick drying property, will dry these paints to useless hardness. One advantage is that they can be painted on to virtually any surface—cardboard, plastic, wood, plaster, paper of any kind. Probably the best solution to the paint problem is to use powder colour in conjunction with an additive (U.K. Marvin). It is supplied in modest sizes and also in gallon cans. It is a proprietary solution which has the effect of retaining the brilliance of the paint so that it does not dry dull and lighter in tone; instead it retains the luminous quality that paint has when wet. Some additives also act as fixatives so that the paint is

6a Powder colour tray   **fig. 6b** Tray with blocks

bonded very securely to the paper or board upon which it is painted.

Similar PVA binders are supplied by other schools supply firms and colour manufacturers, Rowney's' 'PVA Binder' for instance.

Pastel
This is a brilliant medium, easy to store and handle, and inexpensive. It is a dry medium. It must be sprayed with a fixative if the finished work is to be preserved or handled. Children sometimes complain of the dusty effect! It is a medium which is underexploited and undervalued.

Oil pastel
Another newcomer to the painting range, this has all the qualities of pastel and the additional advantages of extra luminosity and brilliance. Also it is dustless. Its main disadvantage is that it is rather expensive.

Poster colours
A moist semi-solid version of powder colour; finer in texture and so much more expensive that it is not an economical proposition for general use in junior/elementary school.

Papers
One of the most expensive items in the school budget is paper, especially art paper. This commodity need not be such a charge on the finances as it often is. It is sometimes quite difficult to dispose of large quantities of waste brown wrapping paper. Why not use it for painting on if funds are low? Better still use newspaper. It is very satisfactory for painting with powder colour, tempera blocks, oil pastel and especially acrylic paints. In fact painting on newspaper offers certain advantages over more expensive papers. One of these is the fact that the child painter may feel persuaded

fig. 7a Blue collage

fig. 7b Picasso

fig. 8   Red snake charmer

fig. 9 Newspaper painting by 10-year-old

fig. 10 Palettes

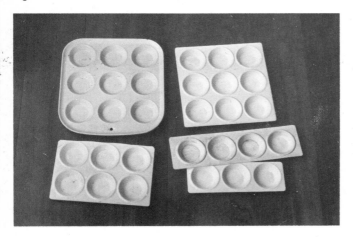

by the need to cover up the printed text and pictures, to make special efforts to use paint rich enough and thick enough to do this. This results in vital paintings. On the other hand I have seen most beautiful textural effects in children's paintings where the type has been allowed to show through.

Another significant advantage of using newspaper is that the pupil is not inhibited by the thought of waste or expense if he makes several false starts and wants to scrap his work and begin again. It is probably true to say that painting on newspaper is an acquired taste for junior/elementary children, but once accepted results can be very satisfactory.

The important requirement for paper which is to be used for colour work is that it should be of sufficient body to allow vigorous brushwork. In Britain we have 'brushwork paper'. Obtainable in off-white and various colours, it is much less expensive than heavy drawing paper and very suitable for any kind of colour work.

Brushes

The basic tool for the application of colour is the brush. Most generally useful in the junior/elementary school are two sizes and types: (1) Good quality hog-bristle, round ferrule, size 12, and (2) good quality sable-blend water colour brushes size 6. These two will cover most needs. It is not wise to economize on brushes. Cheap brushes disintegrate rapidly, and in any case will not do the job they are intended to do. In the end they are dearer than the better quality brushes.

Palettes

The most convenient kind of palette for use in the junior/elementary school is the 'bun-tin' (U.S. muffin tin) type (see fig. 10). Larger ones have 9 or 12 compartments. The smaller type have four. Both can serve as mixing palettes. These two, plus waterjars and the brushes suggested above, are the basic essential tools for work with paint.

Postscript to colour section
When planning school outings remember that some colour manufacturers welcome parties of visitors.

4 The elements of art

Texture

If colour, as one element of art, can be used in this educational way the other elements can too. What are the others? They are Texture, Pattern, Form, Line, Shape. Let us begin with 'Texture'.

The previous section considered a number of different aspects of colour and suggested ways of helping the child to develop his *colour* sense. Texture also is a component of the environment. Sometimes its presence is sensed rather than perceived.

Look at the montage of textures in fig. 11. It would be possible to recognize these by either sight or touch. A great deal of our man-made environment is created by designer craftsmen who need to be able to judge the textural quality of materials of all kinds so as to produce a chair, a radiator, a fur coat, a candlewick bedspread, a car interior, a door mat, a fitted cupboard, a woven carpet or any other commodity, not only so that it functions well, but so that the aesthetic qualities of the materials used shall be elegant and appropriate.

The very young child is highly conscious of textures. He greatly enjoys sliding his hands over the smooth, cool surface of the formica table top; he equally loves the furry feel of his teddy-bear. These are instinctive sensual reactions.

At 9 or 10 years of age sophistication will have set in and pupils will begin to make considered choices; they will take great care in choosing for instance the wood with the most attractive graining, or the woven material with the most exciting structure. As soon as pupils become aware or are made aware of textures, situations can be devised which will provide them with opportunities to explore texture in depth by means of finding, and recording, or making textures.

Rubbed textures

Textures may be studied visually and collected, by using the 'rubbing' process. Put a penny beneath a thin paper and scribble on the paper over the penny. The image of the penny appears on the paper. This is a rubbing.

The making of rubbings is a simple skill. Of itself it is a purely mechanical activity. But if every pupil is asked to make, say, three different rubbings about four inches square, and if these are cut out in neat squares and arranged in a line side by side, and if the children are invited to identify the subjects of each, this becomes a test of perception and an exciting exercise in discovery and the linking of concepts: 'The grille of the headmaster's car radiator', 'the frosted glass door', 'the wood grain on the floorboards', 'the wall', 'the asphalt on the playground'.

Let the children collect as many different rubbings of walls as they can; of tree trunks; let them work to a theme.

The educational value of this is that making a collection of say six wall rubbings pinpoints the pupils looking at walls in order to discriminate between them. The developing of visual discrimination about one's environment is a worthwhile aim.

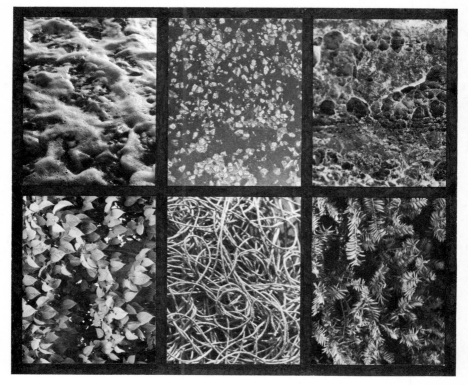

fig. 11   Textures

Drawn textures

Drawn textures are 'made' textures in the sense that they did not exist until the marks were drawn upon the paper.

Figs. 12a, b, c, d show a number of linear textures produced from straight lines, curved lines, scribble, crosshatching.

Figs. 13a, b, c show drawn textures
made from dots, stars, geometrical
forms.

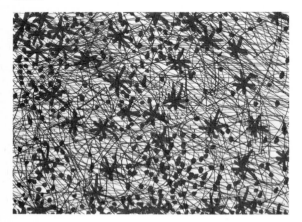

Fig. 14 shows one made from a
combination of all of these. Children
enjoy experimenting with textures.
They often show remarkable powers
of invention when working in this
way.

Fig. 15 shows a group work being
made up from 7-in modules produced
by different pupils.

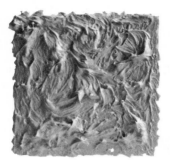

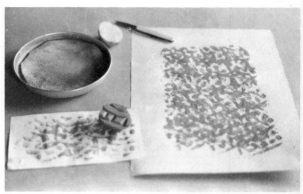

fig. 16   Smooth and impasto paint textures

fig. 17   Texture made with potato

Painted textures

It is possible to 'draw' with paint and brush. It follows that the exercise described above could be carried out by using brush and thin paint to produce drawn textures.

In contrast to this, *thick* paint such as oil paint, PVA, or in junior schools powder paint mixed thickly, can be used to make a paint texture by building up an 'impasto' or 'crust' of paint all over the surface of the painting.

When working with pupils and talking to them about the techniques of painting, suggest they make two patches of paint of the same colour side by side on a piece of paper about 16×20 in. Let the first patch be as smooth as possible and the second as crusty as they can get it. Then discuss with them the difference in appearance, and, when it is dry, the difference to the touch (fig. 16).

Any number of different paint textures may be produced by varying the method of application and the tool used to apply the paint. Let them try this out. Experiments of this kind will give them new techniques and will enrich all their art work.

Printed textures

The texture in fig. 17 is made by the well-known method of 'potato-cut'. The potato block is shown beside it, and also the simple foam rubber tin-lid inking pad. Any block printing technique can be used to make textures, lino block, string block, cardboard block, crumpled paper. The block is simply overprinted in random fashion. See Basic Skills section, page 114.

The drawn, rubbed, painted and printed textures considered so far are all graphic textures. Some kind of medium and a means of applying it is needed in order to produce them: pencil, wax crayon, paint, ink. But textures can also be made, and in fact are made, commercially, by various

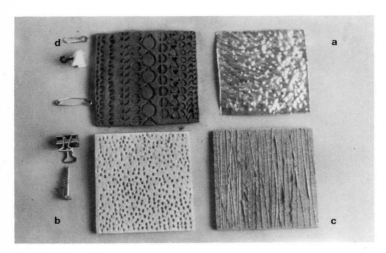

fig. 18a, b, c, d

means, because architects, cabinet-makers, designers, dressmakers, builders and the rest are aware of the important part played by texture in conditioning the appearance of things they produce.

Made textures

Figs. 18a, b, c, d are examples of the way in which surfaces can be manipulated to provide a textural feel and appearance. Fig. 18a is a piece of tin plate which has been hammered, fig. 18b is a piece of wood which has been holed with a punch, fig. 18c is a piece of hardboard which has been scored with a knife. Fig. 18d shows textures impressed in soft clay and the items used to make the impressing. Junior children find the creation of such textures exciting and absorbing.

Found textures

The illustration in fig. 19 is of shallow, 6-in square paper trays made by junior children and filled with materials which they collected. They are dead montbretia (U.S. e.g. Spanish iris) leaves, corrugated cardboard, reed stems, slit bamboo. In my view these look beautiful. A superb wall relief-panel was made, and, hanging in the classroom, it excited much comment from children and adults alike. The collecting provided great excitement and a good deal of natural history as well.

The roundel illustrated in fig. 20 is made of every conceivable kind of granular commodity obtainable from the grocery shop: peas, beans, rice, lentils, and so on.

A good approach to becoming acquainted with textures is to limit the materials used; to say, 'Let's see how many different linear textures we can make from paper.' 'Let's see how many different granular textures we can

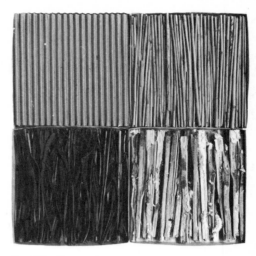

fig. 19 Trays of textures

make'; and 'Let's see how many different textures we can make from wood' (i.e. chips, strips, sawdust, shavings, scored pieces, etc. etc.). Try placing textured items on a tray, and under a cloth. Let the children feel but not see them and let them guess what they are. Some textures are in inaccessible places. The camera can be useful in such cases. Every junior school should have a camera and children should be shown how to use it.

fig. 20

Texture is as universal as colour. The teacher does not have to be a practising artist to interest children in texture. The teacher who is sensitive to surface qualities in the environment is an enriched person. She/he will recognize opportunities for involving the children in 'textural experiences'. The sections above only scratch the surface and point the way. The subject is limitless and bristling with educational activity for the child.

fig. 21a   Zebra

fig. 21b   Pebble

fig. 22   Aerial photographs

fig. 23   Grown pattern

Pattern

The reader would find it interesting to consult a reliable dictionary for definitions of the terms colour, texture, pattern, etc. which form the subject of this section. The definitions given are only conclusive when taken in common contexts. When dealt with in the art sense they become imprecise. Of 'pattern', for instance, the Oxford Dictionary says it is: 'decorative design as executed on carpet, wallpaper, cloth, etc.' No artist would accept this as a satisfactory definition. One of the difficulties in writing about art is that it is a visual subject and verbal equivalents are unsatisfactory. So one must proceed by references.

Is a zebra patterned, or plain? . . . does it conform to the 'decorative design as executed on a carpet' definition? What is the difference between a 'design' and a 'pattern'? Has the concept of 'pattern' somehow got mixed up with 'repeating patterns'?

The marking of the zebra is quite clearly not a repeating pattern, but it

fig. 24   Architecture pattern

is a good example of what most artists understand by pattern, which is the dividing up of the total area within the outline into recognizably defined shapes of either tone, or colour, or texture; in the case of the zebra the pattern consists of irregular alternate bands of black and pale yellow. Think of other animal patterns. Encourage the children to help. Show them, if possible, a tortoise-shell cat, a tortoise, a snake, pebbles with dark and light areas, aerial photographs, plants such as the Coleus, the Anthurium, a Red Admiral butterfly, a Friesian cow.

Man uses pattern as decoration or embellishment. Folk art, ceremonial decoration and heraldry all evoke images of pattern in use. The gardener makes beds of roses and borders of michaelmas daises and green lawns. In other words he divides up the garden into patterns of colour. The architect uses pattern arrangements of white stucco, red brick and timbering. A flag is a pattern.

The simple colour exercise discussed in page 20 was in fact an exercise in pattern-making using yellow paint. Fig. 25 shows a pattern abstracted from black and white pebbles. The boys paid a visit to the beach and selected pebbles which looked interesting, took them back to school, and produced patterns from them. Some boys used designs taken from butter-flies. Some took shapes from the architecture in their environment. Fig. 23 shows a pattern which a girl 'grew'. She started with the centre shape and then added bits to it when she felt drawn to do so and fig. 23 is what happened at the end.

fig. 25   Pebble pattern

fig. 26   Polystyrene structure   fig. 27   Flint

Sensitivity to pattern can be developed. When it is developed it can be employed in its own right, or applied to drawing, or in various skills such as print-making, screen printing, designing.

Form

For our present purpose let us separate 'form' from 'shape' and consider form as referring to three dimensions, and shape as referring to two dimensions.

Every child is born with a sense of form. He makes sand castles, digs holes, builds with bricks, nails pieces of wood together and thumps clay into all kinds of shapes.

A sense of form, of the relationship of three-dimensional forms one to another, is a valuable social asset. It contains the germs of sculpture, architecture, design, home-making.

There is never any shortage in the junior school of three-dimensional raw material in the shape of junk: wooden boxes, cardboard boxes, empty containers of every shape, used packing materials, pressed polystyrene packs, empty tins. Waste paper and cardboard can be used to cut, shape and build three-dimensional forms, with the use of adhesives. In this space age the spacecraft and rocket figure prominently in junior school class-rooms. If the children want to make spacecraft, well and good, let them; but is it valid to 'stimulate' them to make spacecraft? The educational point is that the child should gradually build up a sense of awareness of elegant and appropriate relationships of one three-dimensional form to another. A person who is aware of good formal relationships will not be likely to make extreme mistakes in, for instance, furnishing his home by overcrowding it with badly designed furniture of poor texture, colour and proportion.

fig. 28 Grotesque wood forms

Children have a quick eye for the unusual in nature and in the environment in general. If your school is near woods, quarry, beach, river, junk yard, or derelict ground, a discovery trip will bring to light many interesting and provocative forms, especially if, before starting out, the teacher has primed the children with some such expressive word as 'grotesque' (deliberate link with 'vocabulary'), sinuous, amorphous, contorted, rugged, sinister. 'See who can find the most grotesque shape.' Look for flints, roots, sea forms, driftwood, fallen branches, table legs, rusted iron, bits of old motorcar, corroded metal, springs, bones, and so on. Any child who has had his attention focused on material of this kind will look with new eyes at Lipchitz's, Seymour Lipton's, Henry Moore's or Barbara Hepworth's sculpture. Take the 'finds' back to the classroom.

fig. 29 Cog wheel construction   **fig. 30** Cog wheel cast

There may be a garage near your school . . . the owner may be prepared to keep a box of old bits for the boys and girls.

The children will without doubt present the teacher with twigs which look like giraffes, and with flints that look like nuns in habits. This is part of the activity; but don't *begin* from this angle or the educational point may be missed. The object of the exercise is to stimulate awareness of form as form. The giraffes are incidental.

Line

There is no such thing as a line in nature. In fig. 31 A–B is not a line. It is the right side of one shape and the left side of the shape beside it; the end of one area and the beginning of another. Artists invented 'line' and have used it ever since as a convenient descriptive convention.

Line is commonly associated with drawing but it has many more uses besides. It is used as decoration. It is used as a convention to provide diagrams and to describe shapes. Handwriting and script forms are linear. Drawing is a highly complex use of line. It is helpful to the junior child to be encouraged to explore 'line as line' without any other complication.

Once again it is possible to use the 'game' approach. Clear the largest display board in the room, or use an 8 × 4 ft pin board. Cover the board with white paper; gum pieces together if you have no roll of continuous drawing paper. Provide, say, black pastels, or large black grease crayons, *not* both. This activity can begin with half a dozen pupils while the rest of the class is busy with other things; though in my experience before you have been busy for five minutes the rest will become interested and will want to join in. The first pupil begins at the left (or right) side of the board and is asked to draw a straight line from top to bottom.

The next is set the task of also drawing a line from top to bottom near to the first but it must be a line which is in some recognizable way different from the first. Each pupil takes his turn, to draw a line adjacent to the previous, and each must differ from *all* the previous lines. Before very long each new line causes its maker to stop and think very hard; although in fact the permutations of differences are numberless. Each new line calls for a creative act of imagination on the part of its author. By the time the paper is covered a simple but beautiful linear texture will have been created. Its effect upon the room will be as strong as, though different from, last chapter's colour panel. This sort of linear network of black lines on white makes an elegant background for display of other work (fig. 32).

This simple project causes each child to think in a creative way. The game provides the child with total freedom to create within a clearly defined requirement and with a means of exploring and discovering line as such.

It may well be that some participants will be critical of the performance

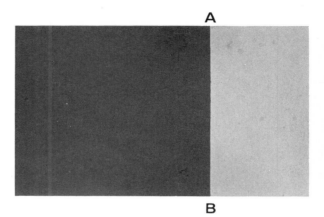

A

B

fig. 31

of others. Some may disapprove of the way others make their lines. It is to be hoped that there *will* be disagreements because this will give the teacher the chance to say, 'All right, take another piece of paper and make lines on that, and you invent *all* the lines.' This provides an open-ended situation. The child who then uses a pastel with a *small* paper will find it less suitable because it produces a comparatively thick line. As a result the size of paper will be brought into consideration. He may find that the line made by a ball-point pen is much more what he wants for his smaller particular purpose. This situation could lead to trying out other drawing media, perhaps bringing together as many different drawing implements as possible.

A development forward from the line game would be to provide as many different drawing media as may be found. In a lively junior/elementary classroom one would expect to find large grease crayons, thin grease crayons, charcoal, felt-tip pens, ball-point pens, drawing pens, fibre-tipped

fig. 32   Typical linear panel

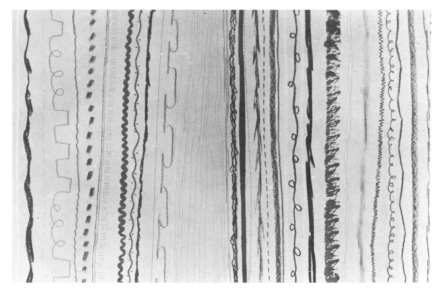

(U.K. Pentel) pens, pastels, pencils of varying degrees of hardness, chalk, conte, brush and paint, brushes of various kinds and ink.

Proceed as before, restricting the exercise to *black*, but this time each participant uses a different drawing implement until all have been used. Then the rota can be run through again. The bright children will realise that a different medium makes the line different anyway. This activity provides the teacher with a valuable opportunity to ply the children with leading questions asking for verbal descriptions of the differences between one line and another.

A third version of the above game is to dispense with drawing altogether and make the lines by stretching differing linear materials from top to bottom; strings of various kinds, wire, raffia, thread, cotton, long thin strips of paper, flex (U.S. light-cord), bindings, pipings, rods, dowels, rolled newspapers, bamboos, stems.

I was visiting a junior school one day and was talking to the lively teacher of a group of children. A 10-year-old girl asked permission to go to the library. I asked whether there were any books about famous artists in the library. 'There's one about Van Gogh,' I was told. 'I'd like to see it,' I said. They rushed off and came back with it, it seemed, in a matter of seconds. I turned the pages asking the children questions about the pictures. Eventually we opened a page at a drawing. 'Do you know what the artist did this with?' 'A pen?' 'Yes, but what sort of pen?' 'What does it say?' They read out 'A reed pen.' What sort of pen is that?' 'A pen made from a reed.' 'What is a reed?' Some discussion about this, then 'It's a sort of tall grass with a feathery bit on the top.' 'Are there any round here?' 'No.' 'Why?' 'They grow by the river' . . . always? Nearly always except they sometimes grow in damp places. 'What colour are they?' 'Green.' 'Always?' 'Green when they are alive, yellow when they are dead.' 'Would the artist use a live one or a dead one?'

By this time most of the class had gathered round and were joining in or just listening. There was lively discussion on the 'live/dead' issue. They ended up by considering he would use a dead one because the live one would be 'too soft and juicy'. 'Is a reed stem hollow or solid?' They were town children and nobody knew. My wife regularly draws with a 'reed' pen and there happened to be one in my car. I fetched it. The children were fascinated to see it. 'Is that really what Van Gogh used to do this picture?' 'It's hollow,' shouted one boy. 'Let's have a go with it, sir.' Ink and paper were fetched and everybody had a try. Then one lad said in a disgusted tone, 'We ain't *got* any reeds . . . so how can we make a pen?' 'It doesn't *have* to be a reed,' I said. 'Have you got any other sort of plants which might do?' 'There's some nettles in the builder's yard' . . . 'there's some michaelmas daisies in our garden' . . . 'there's some docks on the rough grass in the park.' Many ideas were forthcoming.

It was nearly time for the midday meal so at this point the teacher said, 'See if you can find any plants. If you can, bring them back after dinner!' As the children were filing out a lad came to me and said, 'But how d'you make a pen when you have got a reed.' I showed him (see fig. 33).

After lunch a forest of plants and stems was brought into the classroom.

fig. 33   Cutting stems

The teacher initiated a brilliant five minutes' discussion of natural history. The green stems were rejected, the solid stems were set aside and the dead hollow nettle and michaelmas daisy stems were cut to 10-in lengths and the lad to whom I had demonstrated the basic skill of cutting a pen took it upon himself to act as adviser to his friends on how to cut a pen; every child joined in the excitement and before long had provided himself with a pen. They varied in shape and quality, as might be expected, but they all worked. The drawing illustrated in fig. 34 was drawn by one of these children, with a michaelmas daisy stem pen.

This whole exercise, from the first mention of the Van Gogh book, was a good piece of art appreciation achieved by the practical approach of trying out the professional artist's medium and technique, and it linked with natural history and geography.

fig. 34   Reed pen drawing, double portrait. Age 10 yrs.

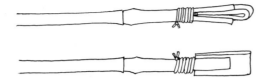

fig. 35b   Stick pen

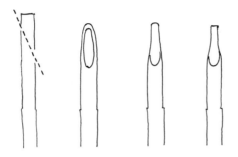

fig. 35c   Bamboo pen

It wasn't long before one of the children found a feather and made a quill pen. The history link was made with the monastic orders and manuscripts.

Children enjoy this kind of activity. The solid stems, or any kind of stick, can be pointed and used as a stick pen (fig. 35b). A desk pencil-sharpener is handy for this! A thin bamboo can be cut in the same way as the reed or michaelmas daisy stem. The bamboo is much more durable (fig. 35c). Thicker bamboo can be split and a wad of felt can be wedged in the split to make felt pens of any width (fig. 35a).

Ink need be no problem. Most education authorities supply ink powders. In any case black and other colour cold-water dyes can be obtained from stores and these, disolved in water, provide excellent inks.

The line game becomes doubly exciting if played with all these unusual new drawing implements. Personal exploration of line on individual papers provides new experiences when all these implements are brought into play.

The activities outlined above will capture the interest of most children and they lead to links with other disciplines. Educationally they lead to sensitivity to line as such. This sort of experience is valuable to the not very able child because it makes no illogical demands upon his ability 'to draw'. All the same, probably the commonest use for line is drawing.

Very many drawing subjects can be seen in terms of line, but by no means all; whereas all drawing subjects can be interpreted in terms of shape. Most drawings contain a combination of line and shape. This brings us to the next element we must consider.

Shape

Shape is virtually inseparable from line. By setting together four lines of equal length, in such a way that they form a four-sided figure, with right angles at the corners, we produce a square. Does fig. 36a consist of 'line' or 'shape'? The word 'silhouette' conjures up a shape of a special kind. Shadow puppets (fig. 36b) depend on silhouette. We recognize friends by their silhouette. Pour a quantity of ink or paint on to a sheet of paper. Watch the shape it assumes. Find a way of repeating that shape . . . and the result is a repeating pattern, Look again at fig. 34. This boy drew his friend's portraits not by drawing lines as lines by by using lines to enclose shapes, by joining all the shapes he could see together; and by relating all the shapes to one another.

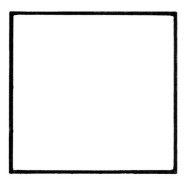

fig. 36a Line square   **fig. 36b** Puppet silhouette

Look round you as you read this. You will see shapes everywhere; not just the shapes of objects but shapes *between* objects. If you can *see* shapes you will be able to set them down on paper. If you can set them down, and put them together, making use of line to do so, then you can draw. (See *You can Draw,* by the same author, Studio Vista, London, and Watson-Guptill, New York.)

Fig. 37a shows a drawing by a junior/elementary boy, which he made after looking carefully at the shapes in his bicycle which he brought into the classroom. When confronted with the suggestion of drawing his bike he flatly asserted he could not do it. 'All right,' said the teacher, 'see if you can just do the shape made by the back fork, bottom bracket and saddle-bar' (marked A). This the boy did fairly easily. Then he was persuaded to add shape (B) and then (C). Gradually he ceased protesting, became absorbed and produced the remarkable drawing in fig. 37a.

This visual isolation of shape, and the relating of one shape to another, is the basic skill of drawing at its simplest.

Colour, texture, pattern, form, line and shape are the basic elements of

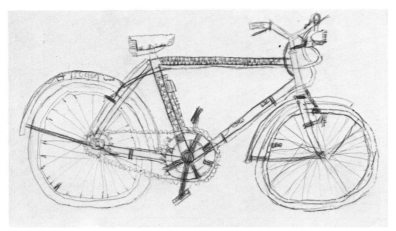

fig. 37a

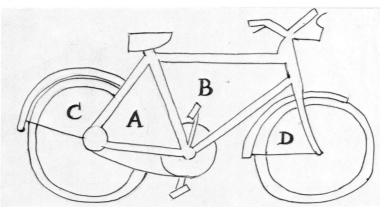

fig. 37b

the artist's visual vocabulary. It has been the aim of this text, so far, to separate out these six elements and to try to show their relevance in the education context and to demonstrate the unique experiences which exploration of them can provide for the children. The child who has been involved in these experiences will have stored up artistic capital in his aesthetic bank. His sensitivities will have been sharpened and he will find it easier to take creative initiatives in the use of art and craft media.

While working with teachers who teach the 7 to 11 age group, I have found their greatest difficulty is caused by lack of knowledge of the basic elements of the subject.

The catalogue of 'basic elements' above began with 'colour' and ended with 'line' and 'shape', the two most closely allied with drawing. This leads us to consideration of drawing as such.

As we proceed constant reference will be made to the six elements. They are all closely interlinked.

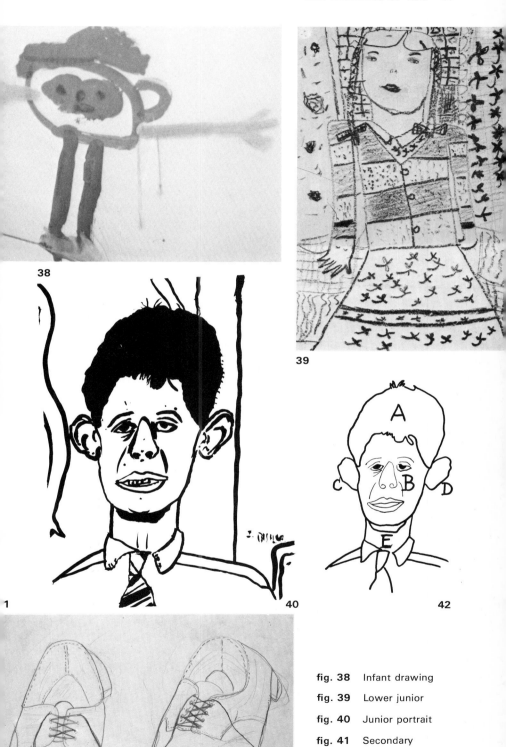

38

39

1

40

42

fig. 38   Infant drawing

fig. 39   Lower junior

fig. 40   Junior portrait

fig. 41   Secondary

fig. 42   Key to fig. 40

5. Drawing

The emancipation of art in schools is still recent enough for there to be lingering memories of the practices which used to pass for drawing; the highly academic, photographically accurate representations of buckets, the 'shading', the copying of plaster casts of acanthus leaves and the like. The attitude of some teachers today to drawing in junior school is highly coloured by such memories. It is also bedevilled by lack of any clear definition as to what drawing is. Ask your artist friends to define drawing and see how they will differ. Look it up in the dictionary.

Figs 38, 39, 40 and 41 show four drawings. Each is a personal statement by its author, yet each is different in idiom. The infant (fig. 38) uses line and mark as symbol into which she builds her own fantasy. The first junior (fig. 39) makes a statement about decoration in simple but formal terms. The second junior (fig. 40) makes an analytical statement about his friend. The secondary pupil says, in line (fig. 41), this is the way my shoes are constructed.

It is probably true to say that fig. 39 is typical of the 8-year age range and that fig. 40 by the 10-year-old is typical of the more mature child. Certainly fig. 40 is a more adult approach; seeking, as it does, to analyse

Line drawings   **fig. 43**   **fig. 44**

fig. 45

and state in simple terms aspects of the world around. The boy has done this by looking very closely at the shapes that go to make up the appearance of his friend. Compare the key diagram with the portrait in fig. 40. Look at (a) and note how this shape is clearly seen and set down by defining the shape of the hair as seen from the front. This shape was put down first by using a line to make the shape and then by filling the shape in with black. The next shape (b) was defined by the line of the temples, cheeks and chin. The ear shapes (c and d) were added; the neck (e), the shirt collar (f), and so on. Each was seen as a shape, and was then defined by lines. The result is a statement in terms of related shapes, about a face, and defined by line.

Many subjects can be interpreted in line. Some subjects lend themselves more naturally to linear treatment than others. A bicycle (fig. 37a), for instance, is more linear than an elephant. The railway lines at Crewe Junction are more linear than the Sahara desert. The head of a young girl with long flowing hair is more linear than the bald head of an old man! Pithead rigs are more linear than slag heaps. A watch interior is more linear than a horse chestnut. Figs 43, 44, 45 show examples of drawing in terms of line.

Drawing as defined above, is a highly expressive art medium, in its own right. It is flexible and, a considerable advantage from the school point of view, it is inexpensive. It is a way of training the eye, and of promoting

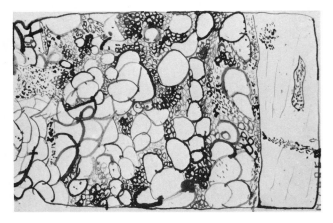

fig. 46 Bubbles in a glass jar

visual and muscular co-ordination. It is flexible in that it can be practised in ball-point pen on a small paper 2 in square; it can equally well be carried out on a large scale, 20 × 4 ft, on the large display board using a 1-in wide felt and bamboo pen. Pupils of this age vary greatly in their tastes as to scale. They should be given a choice, and to allow this, various sizes of paper should be provided.

fig. 47 Trees (stick pen)

Drawing is a basic skill which can be taught and which can be learned. Above all it is a basic skill which brings the craftsman, whether he be junior school pupil, or adult, face to face with his environment. and with his own creative self. It focuses his vision and pinpoints his looking.

A modest facility in the use of line as drawing provides a graphic language for the communication of ideas and experiences of all kinds.

fig. 48a   Cardboard viewfinder

Using a viewfinder

One of the difficulties experienced by draughtsmen, of any age, is that of separating out that piece of the environment they wish to deal with. A simple method of doing this is to use a viewfinder. This is nothing more than a device for enclosing a part of the chosen subject matter, so that the artist may look at it 'out of context'. The viewfinder itself can be a rectangle cut in a piece of cardboard (see fig. 48a) or an old picture frame (fig. 48b).

fig. 48b   Frame and girl friend

Fig. 48a shows part of a bicycle through a cardboard viewfinder. Fig. 48b shows a boy framing his girl friend. In both cases attention is focused upon the shapes within the rectangle. The shapes appear to clarify when enclosed. The profusion of background is simplified. The shapes can then more easily be seen and drawn. Viewfinders can provide openings of any size from one square inch to as many square feet as you like. Suit the viewfinder to the job in hand.

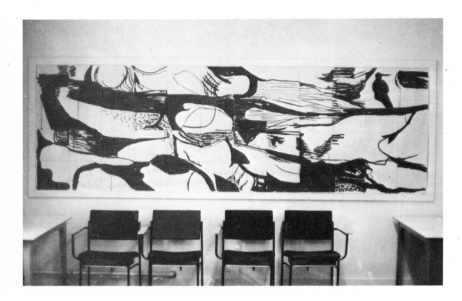

fig. 49 Squared-up drawing *in situ*

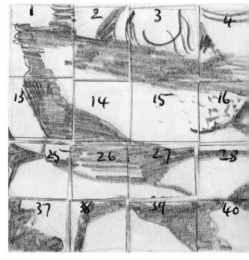

fig. 50 Study squared-up

Enlarging by squaring

Another technique which 10- to 11-year-old children enjoy is enlarging by squaring.

Fig. 49 shows a large drawing carried out by a team of twenty-four junior-school teachers who were taking part in a short course, using the following method. A small study drawing was made by each of the group taking part. When completed these were laid out on table, or floor, and examined, and one was chosen as most suitable for the purpose in hand. In this case the chosen drawing was a study of a piece of tree bark. It was 6 in long by 2 in wide. A grid of $\frac{1}{2}$-in squares was drawn on the study (fig. 50).

Each square was numbered as illustrated and this indicated which way up the square should be. It provided 48 squares in all. The large display board was 12 ×4 ft. That was covered with paper and was also squared up so as to give 48 squares each of which was numbered in the same way and in the same order as the small study; top row, left to right squares 1 to 12; next row down, left to right squares 13 to 24; third row down 25 to 36; and bottom row 37 to 48. The small study was then cut into its individual squares and put in a small box, shaken round, and each teacher chose one piece. Brush and either ink or paint were provided. Each teacher then reproduced the design on his $\frac{1}{2}$-inch square in the square of the same number on the large board. When he had done this he chose another small square and painted that into its appropriate place. When all the squares had been used the large design was complete.

Care must be taken to ensure while working that the small square is held in such a position that the serial number is at the top, otherwise the continuity of the large design will break down.

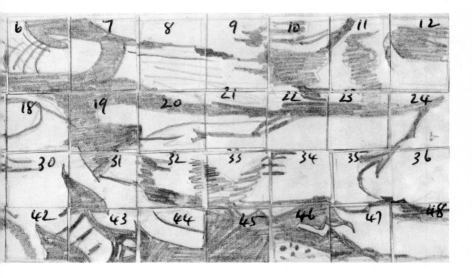

This activity, again, has the character of a game. There is a quality of magic about it which fascinates adults and young alike. It also has valuable links with maths, interior design, and social integration. It is a process well within the capabilities of the 10–11-year-old children, as experience has shown. A stimulating variant on this is to cut a clipping from a newspaper or magazine photograph.

6 Autumn Frieze

fig. 51   Montage of trees in school grounds

A group of 11-year-old boys found themselves in a new classroom, in a new school, on the first day of a new school year. The classroom walls were white and bare. The display boards were large and a depressing buff colour. Teacher and boys together concluded the room needed some colour to brighten it up. They discussed the problem and decided to use the large display boards not for display, but to transform into large panels of colour, and to see what effect that would have on the dull interior. After some differences of opinion it was agreed that yellow would make the brightest colour contribution to the room. The area of the display board was measured and when this was divided into equal 'plots' it was found that each boy would need to cover about 30 × 20 in of paper with yellows in order to cover the whole of the display board surface. It was decided to use paper for the work rather than to paint directly on the display board.

The boys set to work each to completely cover his own paper with the best and clearest yellows he could mix. When the paint had dried the yellow papers were fastened with a staple gun to the display board.

They were made to fit exactly, each overlapping its neighbour slightly, so that no dull board showed through. In addition, the papers were gummed together at the edges so that the total effect was flat and even. The operation was completed in about an hour and a half. The effect was electrifying. The impact of the yellows was powerful and brilliant. The boys were amazed at the result and said it made the room look as though it was 'lit

up by the sun'. There can be no doubt about the power of the colour experience, or that they had 'cheered up' the room. In fact, they had changed their environment for the better. The teacher used this opportunity to say a word about the work of the interior designer. Children from other classes came in, or were brought in, to see the 'yellow'. Its effect echoed through the school.

When the yellow panel had been in position for about a week, a boy said 'but it isn't a *picture* . . . not like that one', pointing to the well-known reproduction of *Poplars* by Cézanne (Venturi 338) which was hanging on the classroom wall. 'I don't like that one,' (the Cézanne) says another boy, 'you never see trees as straight as that!'

The first boy was asked why he thought the Cézanne was a 'picture' and the 'yellow panel' was not. 'Well,' he said, 'you can see what it *is*, it's *trees*.' 'You can see what *ours* is . . . it's yellow!' This raised a laugh. 'It'd look better if it had trees.' 'Well, why not,' said the teacher, 'and,' he pointed out, 'there are plenty of trees in the school grounds.'

The school was very fortunate in this respect. It was only four miles from the centre of London yet it had a big area of grass dotted with trees of various species.

The boys crowded round the windows, and the first speaker said 'There you are; none of those are straight!' 'Some are straighter than others,' said the teacher. These random comments developed into a discussion of

fig. 52 Autumn Frieze (20 ft × 4 ft)

the various growth rhythms of the trees. Some had snaking branches; some curved upwards, some down; some had double curves. At this point the teacher reintroduced the previously made suggestion that trees should be added to the yellows. 'How many shall we do . . . where shall we put them?' The teacher pointed out that it would be a pity to spoil the 'yellows' by putting trees in the wrong place.

As mentioned previously, it was a new school. The new stock of materials had just arrived. There was a pile of large sheets of dark brown wrapping paper. 'Why not cut the trees out of the paper?' suggested the teacher. 'Then you could move them about on the "yellow". And when you get them where you think they look good you can stick them down.'

The class divided itself into twos and threes, and looked out of the windows. They compared the shapes of the trees they could see in the grounds and cut out tree shapes from the brown paper. This was an exercise calling for a sense of 'line'.

Since the beginning of this project the teacher had remained unostentatiously ready with suggestions of a technical kind, suggestions of basic skills whenever they were needed. His method was not to direct, but to suggest, to hold a light rein on the enthusiasm of the pupils. His suggestion to cut out rather than paint the trees was a case in point. The teacher made this suggestion to help the next step in developing the work, but also in the knowledge that if the boys were able to move the trees about on the yellow this would provide an opportunity to bring in a discussion on 'composition' in simple terms. Some elementary aspects of composition are dealt with in the Basic Skills section at the end of the book.

It took a long time to cut out the trees, but finally they were finished.

The yellow panel was taken from the wall and laid on the floor. The 'composition' of the trees began. Again the teacher interposed with the word 'composition'. 'I thought composition was writing,' said one boy. 'Not just writing; more like arranging sentences and paragraphs and words so that they all fit together.' The music parallel was discussed; notes and phrases and movements linked together within an overall shape.

There was vehement discussion in the matter of composing the trees. Children have uncanny skill in fitting the component parts of pictures together. They seem to have an instinct about it. Eventually the positions of the trees were agreed. The teacher took no part at all in the placing and sticking of the trees. One boy invented a good method of forcing the resistant brown paper trees to stick down flat. He removed his shoes and socks and walked along trunks and branches! An effective way of making a collage!

When the gum had set, the Yellow Tree Collage, as it had now become, was re-stapled to the display board, and at this stage it began to look something like the illustration in fig. 52.

The picture was now part of the life of the class and knots of boys chatted about it, on and off, a good part of the time. The next talking point was the fact that all the paper trees looked the same all over . . . 'What about the trunks, and the wrinkles and ridges on the trunks.' Again the teacher was ready with technical advice which would show the way a little further ahead for the boys, in their own personal way, to explore and find. He introduced the device discussed earlier, the 'viewfinder'. This time it was made from cardboard with a rectangular hole cut in it; see fig. 53.

A number of viewfinders were quickly made, some small ones for small

fig. 53

detail. Large ones were used for the tree trunk texture problem at which the boys had just arrived.

The total shapes of the trees cut out of dark paper had been seen and executed from a distance, through the classroom window. In order to see the markings and the texture on the trunks, it was necessary to go out into the school grounds and look at the trunks at close quarters. They carried out this close scrutiny by pinning their viewfinders to the tree trunks. On separate sheets of paper, supported by boards or stiff-backed books, they then drew the shapes and cracks and dark and light patches which made up the trunk textures (see fig. 55). Then they took their 'studies' back into the classroom and added the textures to their own tree trunk in the big picture on the wall (see fig. 54).

They found that the translation of their drawn textures called for consideration of the suitability of the media they used. The first drawings of the textures, on the spot, were made mainly with pencil or diluted ink. These were ineffective on the dark paper of the large design. Black grease crayons were found to be more powerful and more satisfactory. Other media were also experimented with, and this provided useful experience which can only accrue through practice, and trial and error.

Some of the boys had drawn the stark black and white of the silver birches . . . some had taken the less highly contrasted green and yellow patches of the plane trees. Others had drawn the pitted surface of the oak and still others the crazy-paving effect of the horse chestnuts. They translated their own texture motifs very freely, as will be seen from the detail in fig. 54.

Some boys found the task of drawing a texture all over the large trunks rather taxing. The effect looks repetitive rather than creative. But their

fig. 54 Details of textures on trunks

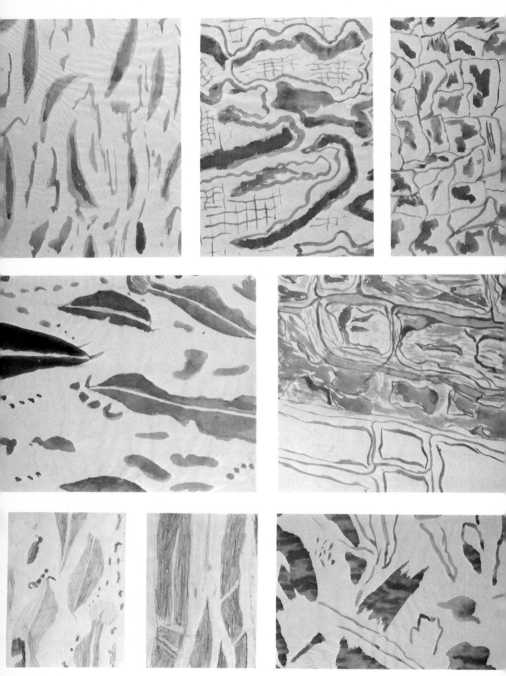

fig. 55 Original trunk studies

making of the original study drawings had helped to form a new way of looking at things. All through that period of the work one heard excited exclamations as their visual explorations revealed, one after the other, new and surprising discoveries. These boys had passed these trees very many times before, yet for the first time, and as a direct result of this project, they were now becoming aware of differences in tree character; the varying growth rhythms of the branches and trunks, the varying colours and textures of the trunks. This new awareness was an enriching experience and might well colour their looking at trees in general in future, and might spread to other 'areas of looking'.

Then followed another period of non-production until one morning somebody said, 'What about the leaves? It ought to have leaves.' Somebody hit on the scheme of going out to collect leaves and then stick real leaves to the trees in the picture. The teacher, privately, guessed this probably would not work but said nothing. Somebody said, 'If it's autumn some leaves will be on the ground.' That was agreed, and they set to work. Very soon however the leaves began to dry and curl up. The boys found them too resistant and brittle to stick on. Some of the class became frustrated. 'Perhaps,' suggested the teacher, 'it would be better to make leaves out of paper! They would stick down all right.' This was tried and found to work. Interest bloomed again. The teacher seized the opportunity and suggested that each one should be a different shape and colour. The collections of leaves were tipped out on to the floor, and others were collected. Enthusiasm mounted once more. The boys were astonished to find so many different shapes, patterns, textures, colours, accidental variations and species. They needed no encouragement to sort them into families, to name them after identifying them. They were fascinated to find, for instance, that every oak leaf is different. To the tired adult this means nothing—to the young child coming to it for the first time it has a touch of the miraculous.

The boys showed remarkable inventiveness in making leaves. Some drew them on white paper, cut them out and painted them. Some painted them and then cut them out. Some cut them out of brown paper. Some used real leaves to print with on paper and then cut out the prints. Others used ink rollers to roll over paper placed on leaves and then cut out the imprints. Some made leaf rubbings. The teacher did not attempt to dissuade the boys from using the leaves as templates to draw round. They did so and the resulting outlines were then filled in with paint. Identification of leaf species is by means of shape. The link between art and natural history is clear.

All the boys now had collections of paper leaves and they set about adding a collage of leaves along the foot of the *Autumn Frieze*, and individual leaves elsewhere over the picture surface.

The planned and the unexpected

In every teaching situation there are two concomitants, the known and the unknown; the planned-for result, and the unexpected opportunity for dialogue, and development of ideas, which arises out of the work the child is doing.

The unexpected may be initiated by either child or teacher.

The known, planned-for, results of the yellow tree panel project have

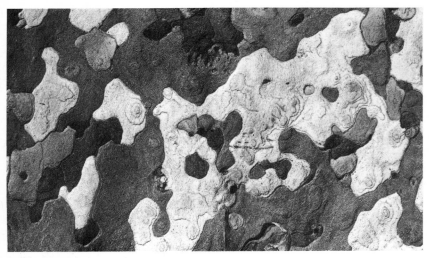

fig. 56 Plane tree abstract

fig. 57 Boy's wood carving   fig. 58 African figure

already been stated. The teacher and children together had in mind the brightening and decorating of the classroom. The teacher had in mind (1) to expose the boys to an activity which could be expected to sharpen their sense of colour, (2) to stimulate and focus their visual appreciation of the structure of the trees in their environment, (3) to use their sense of *line* to do this, (4) to engage their sense of pattern and shape by structuring a situation which would call for differentiation between the various species of leaves, and (5) to test their visual reaction to texture by providing them with a means of abstracting the markings on the trunks and applying them in the context of their own group picture. All these were planned, in advance, by the teacher. They were foreseen as situations which could lead to rewarding experiences of an educational kind. In addition, and very importantly, a number of unplanned though not entirely unexpected openings presented themselves. They are listed below.

As one boy looked at the plane tree trunk he observed that it looked like 'modern art, like in that book in the library'. When they arrived back in the classroom the teacher suggested he should fetch the book. It turned out to be a copy of *Picasso* by Gertrude Stein (Batsford, London, 1938) which had been bequeathed to the school library (fig. 56)

He searched through and finally stopped at Plate 32, *Nature Mortes aux Lettres Russes, 1914*. 'Let's have a look,' said three of his friends, as the teacher and he were studying it. The boy explained that Picasso's forms reminded him of the plane tree trunk, or vice versa; the three friends immediately asked for permission to go and look at the tree. They came back, agreeing with their friend, and that much richer for having acquired a new cross-reference between forms in the natural world and the unfamiliar forms of a great creative artist.

Another boy, while wandering round the grounds, found a small branch lying beneath a tree. He brought it back into the classroom, saying he was going to make something out of it. After a determined battle, with penknife, mount-cutting knife, a small hacksaw, a rasp, and a saw, he finally produced the figure in fig. 57.

He was a boy whose gifts tended to be practical rather than academic. His carving attracted a good deal of praise. The teacher had at home a Nigerian wood sculpture which showed how the artist had used the curvature of the branch (fig. 58) to aid the form of the figure.

The boy's crude figure now assumed greater status in the eyes of the rest of the class and led to exploration of African sculpture in the school and local library. (*Primitive Art* by Douglas Fraser; Thames & Hudson, London; Chanticleer Press, N.Y., 1962—is useful.) A visit was paid to the Horniman Museum to see the real thing! This experience of sculpture also led to a link with geography and map-reading and to discussions about why the African sculptures were made; to voodoo; and to talks about why religion is not the same in all countries. A remarkable and beautiful film on Indian folk art which included wood carving and sculpture was hired and shown to the children—its title *Kaleidoscope Orissa*, made by Mary Kirby for Pilgrim Films, London, and distributed in U.K. by Gateway Educational Films Ltd, Green Lanes, Palmers Green, London, N.17.; U.S. Distributor: International Film Bureau Inc., 332, South Michigan Avenue, Chicago, Illinois 60604.

There was an amusing sidelight on wood carving. One of the trees in the grounds was descriptively carved with a fine display of hearts, arrows and initials, indicating a web of amorous intrigue. The boys' comments about these were made with typical Cockney directness and lack of inhibition. This, too, was turned to use by the teacher who pointed out the possibility of danger, especially to young trees, if the trunks are ringed. This led to a new tour of the grounds to see if any of the trees had been cut. None had, but there was one dead tree. The cause of death was not apparent, and this set the boys enquiring of another teacher. They went to him because he had the best knowledge of natural history. The episode

fig. 59 Distorted tree graft

also provided an opportunity to discuss some elementary aspects of town planning and environmental architecture, especially in the context of London's planning policy, whose council have a proud record of preserving every possible tree in the city to provide amenity. One school was partially designed round a fine mulberry tree. Shortly after it was completed the mulberry tree died. The unusual shape of the school is a continuing puzzle to those who see it and do not know the story. Such architects are on the side of the angels.

A piece of bark was hanging loose on one tree. A boy pulled it away and found underneath a colony of small insects. This called for another visit to the science teacher, who helped the boys to look up and identify the leather-jackets and talked to them about the life cycle of the daddy-long-legs.

The tree in fig. 59 shows one of the trees in the grounds of the school which attracted the boys' attention because of its odd shape. It happened that the school caretaker was a keen gardener and he explained that this tree, early in life, had been produced by taking a vigorous standard stem and grafting a frailer species into the top by the 'hole and spike' method, and that it had been in the ground a very long time and gradually the delicate graft had grown in strength and had finally outgrown its host. The result can be seen in the illustration. The group of boys to whom he spoke were fascinated. They took away from that impromptu discussion germs of ideas which could well proliferate and lead to creative activities in gardening later in life. From this episode a lively conversation developed about 'uncles who bud roses' and 'brothers who had skin grafts' . . . and about whether heart transplants 'worked that way'?

Economics of wood

Some of the trees had been lopped earlier in the year and this raised again the discussion on 'not spoiling the trees'. This was opposed by the opinion that 'you can't have branches falling on your head. Trees have to be made safe.' The discussion ranged to felling trees, cutting trees up to make planks, cost of timber and uses of timber; how one type of timber can be distinguished from another when it is in plank form. They saw the point that identifying a plank of wood is rather like looking at an abstract painting—the criteria are colour, line, texture. Weight and density were considered. This part of the project was greatly helped by a teacher who had a friend who was head of the handicraft department of a large school and who recommended *What Wood is That?* by Herbert A. Edlin, and *Mechanical Properties of Timber* by F. D. Silvester, as good books to consult on the subject. The first of these contains actual samples of a large number of different woods.

Another valuable sideline came out of the *Autumn Frieze* project. A teacher with English as his main college subject helped in this. He and the art teacher compared notes and used the same leading-question technique as that used to stimulate the 'seeing' of the trees for the art work. The following are two examples of creative writing produced by junior children after this sort of stimulus.

A rough and soft bark, it was a combination of dark brown and a reddish brown with a few pale orange parts, all of this was covered slightly with silvery grey specles. The bark was rather dull and the orange parts felt of velvet, it all together smelt of dust. The bark was in sections with large gaps between each one. The sections were very brittle and broke easily.
(*Boy age 11*)

The tree in summer

The trunk is grey
With fawn peeping here and there
Mid-brown is with the grey
Silver takes a look out
Dark fawn is round the edge.

The trunk is like a rhions [rhino's] skin,
All bumpy everywhere
The bark is blunk and rotting here and there
A smell of nature is the smell
And a kind of moss grows up.

The bole is big and bumpy
And gose under the ground
The nature smelling trunk

Gose up till it stopps
And branches spred out
With green leaves hanging.

(*Girl age 10*)

It is surprising to find so many junior school teachers who are highly skilled in encouraging their pupils to write creatively about events, ideas, and environment and yet who profess to find difficulty in stimulating the child to paint. In fact the same method of stimulating creative writing, leading questions, direct visual stimulus, stimulus of the imagination, all work equally well for the painting of pictures. Try an experiment. Ask your junior children to produce a piece of creative writing about 'Trees' without any kind of stimulus. Then involve them in using a viewfinder. Let them write a description, as described earlier in the Colour section, of each colour they find. Focus their attention on the trunk textures, the branch rhythms, the characteristics of the leaves and the colour of the backgrounds. After this exposure see whether the children produce more expressive prose. Creative work in paint, and creative writing call for the use of similar faculties and abilities; the medium is the substantial difference. One would expect that similar stimuli should work.

The deployment of teachers in the *Autumn Frieze* project was fortuitous. Cohesion was achieved by the wide-ranging enthusiasms of the central teacher and by his calling upon his colleagues when the boys started a line of thought which linked with another teacher's special subject. Let us list the subjects which in fact integrated with the central theme of 'trees'. They were: art appreciation, wood sculpture, sociology, anthropology, comparative religion, geography, folk art, botany, town planning, environmental design, biology, horticulture, gardening, the economics of timber, creative writing. All these are in addition to the central subject, art, used in its own right to promote sensitivity to colour, texture, line, and shape.

It is interesting to speculate how much more effective this might have been if a 'team-teaching' approach had been used; with a group of teachers positively available to the project and each ready to add his special knowledge and subject emphasis, within the total context. Perhaps 'team-teaching' will be the solution to the problem of providing enough art specialist expertise in the junior school! It should be possible to make sure that the staff of every junior school includes members with qualifications which cover most of the subject areas. This could be achieved if, when staff are appointed, a spread of subjects is sought; i.e. one teacher, with main subject training for English, Geography, History, Art, Physical Education, Science, Mathematics, and so on. They would not teach *only* their main subject. They would still be general teachers but their special knowledge about and their enthusiasm for their main subject would be available in the school, and especially in the staff room, and this would be to everybody's advantage. The value of team-teaching would be lost if every member of the team was, say, an English specialist. Team-teaching will be discussed again.

The *Autumn Frieze* opened doors on a good many inter-connected activities. How much the poorer it would have been if *only* the one teacher had dealt with it instead of bringing in other of his colleagues whom he knew had special knowledge.

How would the project have varied if it had been started by the Science teacher? Would line, texture, colour, composition, pattern, shape, social integration, have come into it? Does this imply that at junior level teachers should not work in isolation? Town planning might have come into it, biology, gardening. But suppose the project had been started and run by the Science teacher without help from colleagues, and suppose, in the groups, there had been a boy with very low ability in science, and great sensitivity to art. Is it likely that boy would have suffered by default?

How would the *Autumn Frieze* project have varied if it had been started by the English teacher, the Maths, Geography, History, teachers?

Work on *Autumn Frieze* was intermittent and lasted well over a fort-night, but eventually the moment came when the last boy stuck the last leaf in place and the last bit of texture was added. The teacher, at this point, drew the class together and started a discussion on whether the picture had achieved its object. Did it make the room look brighter? Was it 'more like a picture' now the trees had been added? The boys agreed unanimously that it was a success as a piece of interior decoration and one boy said, 'And I liked all the other things we did while we were doing it.'

While work was proceeding the boys were involved in discrimination, about creative expression of colour, yellows, and in visual exploration of the school grounds. They were faced with a series of situations, the placing of the trees for instance, which called for a 'problem-solving' approach. They were faced with the necessity of coming to terms with their fellows so that they could work together as a team. They acquired new ways of look-ing which pinpointed and particularised their visual awareness of growth rhythms, textures. They had never really seen those trees before in spite of having looked at them every day on arrival at school.

The value of the *Autumn Frieze* project in terms of education can be stated as follows:

It provided:
1. Increased sensitivity to colour, line, texture, shape, pattern
2. Increased awareness of the environment
3. The development of an attitude of critical appraisal of their own work
4. Critical appraisal of Cézanne's work!
5. The project introduced the pupils to the concept of 'problem-solving'
6. The project provided experience of social integration

All of the above were foreseen by the teacher as likely, and desirable results. In addition there were the many divergent, yet linked, experiences, the gardening, the design, cross-references to art appreciation, sociology, and so on.

The whole project was a partnership between pupils and teacher with the teacher consciously 'structuring' the situation.

'Structuring', by the teacher, far from restricting them, sets the pupils free. It unlocks the doors of the imagination and leads to true creativity.

7 Integrative teaching

The preceding account of the making of the *Autumn Frieze* describes an example of an integrative educational process at work in the school. The term 'integrative process' is used deliberately and in preference to the current overworked word 'integration'. Integration is a vague concept of which a convincing definition has yet to be put forward. Yet, in spite of this, the word is constantly heard in school staff rooms and across the table at education committee meetings. There is a danger of the growth of a specious philosophy that 'Integration is a Good Thing', and so should be imposed 'from the top'. This is unacceptable.

On the other hand integrative teaching can, and does, arise automatically in many good schools when certain conditions obtain; for instance when significant aspects of different subjects overlap and are seen to overlap. Composition as mentioned in the section dealing with the *Autumn Frieze* is a good example. Consider composition in Art and Music and English. The mechanics of composition in these three subjects are basically the same; i.e. the fitting together of subsidiary parts within the total framework of an all-embracing form to provide a balanced, harmonious and satisfying whole.

This type of integration provides the pupil with illuminating views across associated strata of experience. Once this kind of integration is achieved the scene is set for 'combined operations'.

Integrative teaching takes place automatically where teaching staff are compatible and share the same ideas and ideals and who have ability in more than one discipline which share common factors, for instance, Art and Drama. Puppetry links the crafts of puppet-making, scene-painting, handicraft, music, poetry and playwriting, speech development, drama, and possibly tape recording.

Integrative teaching arises where organisation and time-tabling permit free movement throughout the school.

Many old school buildings will be with us for a long time yet. Integration is more a matter of open minds, open doors and open discipline than of open-plan accommodation, though this is not to decry new building, and experimental planning.

Integrative teaching arises naturally where multi-purpose areas are provided, because this enables cross-fertilisation by 'observation and doing' and by 'shared excitement and experience'. It arises where opportunities are sought, and made, to allow the sharing of experiences. Class I went to Westminster Abbey. Some of them in assembly described the visit to the rest of the boys and girls. Paintings of animals displayed in circulation areas enable experiences gained on a visit to the Zoo to be shared. Class IV go through their 'movement' routine for the school to see. Class VI black out the library and use the projector to show to their school-fellows the slides they made without a camera.

The Plowden Committee, which carried out the most comprehensive survey of Primary Education ever attempted in Britain, published its findings and recommendations in 1967. The Report,* in two substantial

* Plowden Report: 'Children and their Primary Schools'. H.M.S.O., 1967 (2 vols.).

volumes, is a major contribution to the literature on English Primary Education. In volume one, paragraph 542, this committee of eminent experts states:

'. . . Integration is not only a question of allowing time for interests which do not fit under subject headings; it is as much a matter of seeing the different dimensions of subject work and of using the forms of observation and communication which are most suitable to a given sequence of learning.'

This is a perceptive, and cool, appraisal. It is significant that the Plowden definition sees integration not as 'The Method', but as a characteristic of good liberal teaching in a good school situation.

Project, theme and centre of interest

It is now accepted that some form of inter-disciplinary approach is desirable at the 7–11 years level of learning. How does the school set about achieving this?

The project, the theme and the centre of interest are familiar patterns of teaching in English junior schools and in other countries. These methods of teaching are a manifestation of the trend towards integrated teaching which sets out to break down the barriers of subject, accommodation, time and age, and which sees the flexible yet 'structured' learning situation which leads in many directions, from one common starting point, as the ideal. Every visitor to a school 'Open-Day' will be familiar with the projects on coal, wool, space, inescapably space, Red Indians.

I recall one remarkable centre of interest which had Inland Waterways (the British canal system) as its theme. It included map-making, bridge-building, natural history, bird migration, engineering, social history. The illustrations, in the main, were somewhat stilted drawings or tracings from books. There was a scale model of a narrow-boat, made from cardboard and paper, which had engaged the boys and girls in elaborate measuring and calculation; but nowhere was there any sight or mention of the characteristic and decorative traditional folk design which was so essential a part of the ethos of nomadic folk who manned these vessels and travelled these waterways (fig. 60).

If the teacher had been able to consult a colleague knowledgeable in art, or if the project had been run by team-teaching, such an omission would probably not have occurred. This example is included, not to suggest there *must* always be an art content in any and every project. It is to suggest that where there is an art content of such obvious value, in any project, it should not be ignored.

A school visit to the Inland Waterways Museum at Stoke Bruerne, Northamptonshire, for those within striking distance, would be a worthwhile undertaking. What better accommodation could there be for integrated studies than a 'narrow-boat' converted to provide a mobile class-room. *A Short History of the Narrow Boat* by Tom Chaplin (17½p) makes stimulating and infectious reading.

There is no doubt about the value of the project, the theme, and the centre of interest, providing it leaves opportunity for the individualist pupil to contract out if he prefers to follow his own, perhaps newly found, private line of enquiry. It is possible for some children to become bored if the pro-ject is not to their liking, or if it is persisted in for too long. Sensitively handled, the project provides many valid and powerful learning situations.

The content and the starting point for projects will depend upon the situation at the time, the interests of the pupils, perhaps even the policy of the school. The strongest single influence will be that of the teacher and his or her subject bias, but, if there are to be subject-centred projects then art must be one of the subjects, and a fair share of the projects must be based upon art, or at the least have art as its point of departure. Some likely starting points might be:

line	texture	architecture	pattern
adornment	ceremonial	display	camouflage
colour	disguise	decoration	structure
drawing	dance	rhythm	exhibition
theatre	folk art	costume	embroidery
the Church	museum study	surrealism	the Impressionists
impressions	tapestry	weaving	walls
arabesque	illumination	wallpaper	jewellery
sparkle	shape	silhouette	surface
webs	contours	badges	spectacle
images	handwriting	symbols	stones
tessellation	glass	dyes	hair
transparency	communication	reflections	magnification
holes	asymmetry	form	mummers
symmetry	straight lines	nets	brickwork
curves	portraiture	light	waves
circles	marble	pattern in	painting
ceramics	mathematical	nature	spots
stripes	patterns	spirals	modelling
filigree	printing		

The above subjects are all based on art, have art links, or are themselves elements of the arts. At first sight some may seem some distance removed from art for the 7–11-year-old children in the classroom. If you feel this, select one of the headings at random and think about it on the way to

fig. 60   Canal barge and details of folk art

school. Look it up in the dictionary and visualize the images evoked by the definitions it gives: talk about it with the children. Let's take one now and see how far it can be developed in a paragraph. Let's try 'decoration', and begin by compiling a list of linked concepts.

In the context of decoration ornament comes to mind: ornament in dress, i.e. national dress, ritualistic costume, ceremonial costume, heraldic uniform, military uniform; ornament on furniture, ormolu, enamel, carving, fretting, embroidery, tapestry; architectural ornament, decorative brickwork, pinnacles, Gaudi, Gothic stone carving, Acanthus leaves, pilasters, pattern, panelling, graining, inlay, tracery, moulding, beading, needle-work, brocade, lace; personal ornament, necklaces, rings, tiara, pompadour wigs; wreath, festoon, garland, bouquet, tassels, epaulettes, rosettes, bows, tinsel, sequins, frills; chasing, filigree, illumination, embossing, tessellation.

All the above words are visually evocative. Each of them signifies an art product, wrought by the exercise of art or craft skills. A theme thus based would involve children in assessing such products, and deciding whether they are 'artistic'. It would test their discrimination, provide exercise in vocabulary and very many opportunities for dialogue.

If the teacher decided to steer the next theme towards the direction of ornament, he might begin by discussing the concepts and by drawing from the class as many ideas as possible, and keeping many relevant ideas in the air. The assortment of words listed above is like a bombardment of visual images. It is not suggested that the teacher should bombard the children, but that discussion should be deliberately used to generate visual imagery through the medium of words in the first place; to build up a kind of verbal saturation which in turn evokes an ethos in which teachers' and children's contributions combine to provide starting points and jumping-off places for creative exploration of all kinds.

Each one of the above words conjures up a series of visual images. Examples can be drawn, written about or painted. Illustrations can be found in books or magazines, actual examples can be brought in or replicas can be made and included in displays. Think of the possibilities of the word 'jewellery' in this context, and of what can be made from clay and wood and paper and wire and beads and sequins and milk-bottle tops, etc.

A glance back over the last few paragraphs will show the possibilities for linking with other subjects; ritualistic costume with geography; military uniform with history; architecture with social studies, to mention only three. A subject such as Ornament, which is basically an art subject, can provide educational studies in both breadth and depth at the same time. In addition the positive, foreseen and planned-for art education result will be an increased awareness of the place and function of ornament and decoration in everyday life, and in geographical and historical perspective.

The well-run project has the effect of linking together many of the diverse components of the curriculum and normal activities of the school. A danger of this is that it is sometimes thought that 'the project' is always equally effective in all areas. This is not inevitably the case. There must be conscious pre-planning of all projects, with the aim of making possible effective experiences for the children, and laying emphasis, in specific areas, geography one time, art another time, but using all possible links all of the time. All projects will produce integrated work but each one will be orientated towards different subjects at different times.

To return to art; the degree of significant art experience provided by any project will vary according to certain factors, and these fall under three main headings:

1. The project on a 'non-art' theme run by a 'non-art' teacher will involve some art, though this is likely to be minimal and superficial.

2. The project on an 'art' theme run by a 'non-art' teacher or alternatively the 'non-art' theme run by an 'art' teacher. Both these situations will provide many art opportunities for both teacher and pupil; and art and craft will be likely to play a vital part in the activity.
3. The project on an 'art' theme run by an art teacher would be most likely to involve the teacher, or teachers, and the children in the most significant and educationally valuable art experiences.*

Autumn Frieze is an example of this kind. In that project experiences which are only possible through art played a main part.

The three alternatives listed above would be less sharply differentiated in a 'team-teaching' situation because an art teacher would always be available. 'Team-teaching', it seems, might well provide a solution of the difficulties and problems of teaching art to children who are in the transitory 7- to 11-year stage.

Creativity

The number of children in the 7–11 age range and more especially the 8–11 range who can start unaided from scratch and proceed to creative activity, in any medium, is not large. In this they do not differ from the adult, or the professional artist. Beethoven, Keats, Hemingway, Matisse, all began with, and needed, the stimulus of powerful experiences—aural, musical, verbal, social, visual, formal—to start them off.

The higher the child goes in the junior school the more he will need precisely considered teacher-administered stimulus. Experience is the chief stimulus. Significant experience will produce significant forms of expression. Significant art experiences will induce the pupil to produce significant art.

The child's sensitivity is the door through which the stimulus makes its impression on his senses. As it penetrates and produces a response so ideas will be generated which will trigger off creative activity.

In *New Horizons in Psychology*, Pelican (Penguin Books, Baltimore), Moya Tyson offers some interesting quotations on creativity which are relevant. She refers to the social psychologist Irving Taylor, who suggests there are 'five levels of creativity' and that basically creativity is 'an approach to problems' rather than the accidental result of professional training!

The first level he quotes, Expressive Creativity, is typical of the spontaneous drawing of the infant (fig. 61a). This, he states, is the most fundamental form of creativity and involves independent expression where skills, originality and the quality of the product are unimportant.

* *Note.* The terms 'art' teacher and 'non-art' teacher are not used in a derogatory way. They are meant to imply in the case of the 'art' teacher one who studied art as a main or major subject while at college and who has special enthusiasm and/or ability in the subject. The term 'non-art' teacher is used in the sense of a teacher with little or no training in art and who accordingly feels ill-equipped to deal with the art content of a project.

figs. 61a-d
'Five levels of creativity'

a

b

c

fig. 61d   Picasso

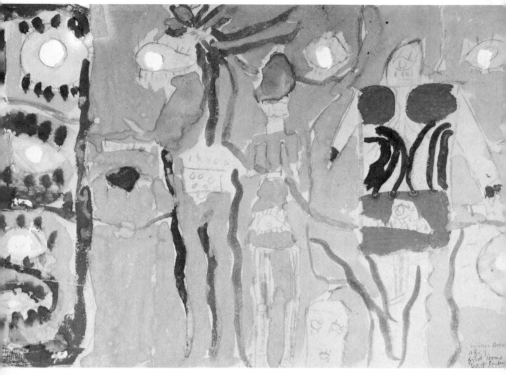

fig. 62   Dream, girl aged 10

The second level he calls Productive Creativity. In it there is a tendency to restrict and control free play and improve technique (fig. 61b). The attempt at realistic representation of a man by a junior child, for instance, displaces the earlier spontaneous and free expressive conception of the infant.

The third level, Inventive Creativity, he suggests involves flexibility in perceiving new and unusual relationships between previously separated parts (fig. 61c).

The fourth level he calls Innovative Creativity, and is demonstrated by few people and involves significantly modifying the basic foundations or principles underlying a whole field of Art or Science, and beyond this, he quotes a fifth level, 'Emergentive Creativity', where an entirely new principle or assumption 'emerges at a most fundamental and abstract level', the Cubist School of Painting for instance. Both levels 4 and 5 it seems to me subsist in fig. 61d, *Seated Nude*, by Pablo Picasso.

The inference which we might draw from the above is that the junior school child of 9, 10, 11 is at the 'second level', productive creativity, that he allows himself less freedom at this stage and looks for improved technique. 'Miss, it doesn't look right. How can I make it look right?'

The highly imaginative child is likely to be highly sensitive, and possibly to require less stimulation than his classmates. He is also likely to be much more rare. The front cover illustration, *Bird*, and fig. 62, *Dream*, are remarkable pictures. *Bird* in particular would seem to belong to Irving

fig. 63 Garden still life

Taylor's 'third level', Inventive Creativity. The child certainly displays 'flexibility in perceiving new and unusual relationships between previously separated parts' of the bird. *Dream* is equally remarkable, in a mystical sense. Not many pictures with this highly individual quality are likely to be encountered at junior school level. The image makers, the third level creators, are probably more frequently to be found at secondary school level.

Needless to say, when a highly gifted child is encountered at junior, or any, level he should be given every opportunity to develop his unique capabilities while at the same time enjoying the standard fare provided for the average child.

Current thinking on the need to teach basic skills at upper junior level would appear to find support, in art at any rate, among some psychologists.

8 Creativity, originality, stimuli, change

There is no doubt that a great deal of spontaneous creativity arises from the activities of a project. The project provides the stimulus. But what about stimuli for the child working alone? Are there different types of stimuli which will start him off?

Visual stimulus

This can be generated in various ways by confronting the pupil with visual phenomena which intrigue, delight and shock him, and especially which challenge his curiosity. What child can resist looking through a microscope; using a hand-magnifying glass. Let him see a slide of, for instance, a flea. He will be amazed at the colour and the strange pattern of the insect seen under the microscope.

Fig. 63 shows a still-life by a girl of 10 years. The items in the group were brought to school by the teacher and set up in the classroom on a background of white paper. Teacher and pupils then talked about the colour and the shapes. These are ordinary everyday things, but they seem different, somehow more magical, when set up in the classroom. The children were not pressed to treat the group as a whole but to state the colours and shapes of the various items individually.

Blow bubbles for them.
Light a small fire on a plate and let them watch the thin smoke drifting across the sun.

Dressing-up is a highly effective stimulus. Every classroom should possess a modest collection of dressing-up clothes. The examples in figs. 64a, b, c show 'a gardener'; father's old waistcoat and hat, a trowel and a plant pot: 'a lady in a flowery hat'; an old sun-hat and artificial flowers made and assembled by the girl wearing it: 'a lady with a sunshade'; a girl in cotton frock posing with open Victorian parasol. Dressing-up provides

figs. 64a, b, c

fig. 65a   Indian

fig. 65b   Girl with parasol

fig. 65c   Spanish lady

fig. 66   Snow-storm

an element of drama and theatre and usually produces amusement and excitement. Figs. 65a, b, c show some pictures resulting from 'dressing-up'.

Coco the clown, in full regalia, visited a junior school to talk to the children about road safety. The clowns painted after his visit were immeasurably more expressive than the hackneyed stereotypes of clowns so often seen. The added vitality sprang directly from the immediate visual impact of Coco's striped baggy trousers, red nose, huge eyebrows, floppy boots and the rest. His bizarre appearance generated great creative fervour. It is the teacher's job to generate creative fervour.

A teacher prepared a large quantity of small flakes of white, very thin tissue paper. He then asked six children to take the biggest handful possible in each hand, and to stand on a long table, in front of the class. Then, with everybody watching, and very curious, they all six simultaneously scattered the small flakes in a thick storm which drifted slowly down to the floor. The visual impact was considerable. What did it make you think of? asked

fig. 67 Hawthorn and birds

the teacher. 'Snow,' said a good number . . . 'a wedding,' said one, 'confetti,' said another. . . . 'Autumn' was another offering. Fig. 66 shows a snow picture produced as a result of this 30-second visual phenomenon.

A highly effective method of providing visual stimulus is to import into the classroom the 'unexpected object' such as a pineapple, a lobster, a skull. Two or three radio valves, clock mechanisms, a bicycle, a madonna lily. The illustration in fig. 69 is by a 10-year-old girl.

Children are intrigued by musical instruments. They can be used as a visual stimulus.

Fig. 70 was drawn by a 6-year-old boy the day after he saw on TV the French version of the Concorde's first take-off. Powerful emotive visual stimulus with delayed action drawn from the TV screen.

The use of the viewfinder has been mentioned earlier especially in connection with *Autumn Frieze*. On that occasion it was used as a means of collecting visual information about the textures on the tree trunks. The viewfinder can also be used in the abstract, as an activity in its own right, not necessarily geared to the production of an 'end-product'. It will be found to be a remarkable stimulus to looking and seeing and exploring visually. Try the experiment of providing the group of pupils with a sheet of stiff paper or card, say 15 × 11 in, and ask the children to cut a rectangular viewfinder out of the centre, say 3 × 6 in. This will leave good-sized margins all round. Let the pupils go out of doors and find a visually interesting surface; it may be a tree trunk, a road surface, a large corroded metal object, a wall. Ask the children to select a visually interesting piece and pin, or hold their card so that they can see their selected piece through it. Now ask

fig. 68 Pineapple

fig. 69 Madonna lily

fig. 70   Concorde, boy aged 6

them to write, down one margin, a list of names of all the colours they can
see inside their rectangle. Next ask them to make a drawing of all the lines,
shapes and textures; suggest another drawing of the light and dark tones.
Ask them to look at, feel and describe the surface of their selected piece of
wall, or whatever they have chosen. Finally, ask them to note down any
signs of life or living organisms, i.e. spider's web, insects, moss, dew. The
examples below are typical.

> I pinned my viewer to a wall. The bricks were hard. The pin would
> not go in at first. It was a yellow wall and had some blue and red.
> The blue was like smoke and the red was dull and spotted.
> The bricks are stuck with morter. Morter is duller yellow still. The
> wall is bumpy when you see it close to. It felt warm because the sun
> shone on it. It has cracks and lots of very little holes. It feels very
> rough like sand paper. One of the bricks had soot on it. The wall
> was made of old bricks.
> There were no animals. There was a fly and some ants and a little
> spider web in a little hole with a dead leaf caught in it. A little green
> weed was growing out of a crack.

> Red grey beige black Light Brown White Rusty Roughish Smooth
> Jagged blunt Fragile in places hard blackish green animals under
> wood. (*words describing tree bark seen through viewfinder; girl 10*)

The first time they are exposed to this activity the children will be amazed
and excited and the experience will be an enduring one. They will have
developed new awareness of, and sensitivity to, colour, texture, tone, line;
they will discover that vegetable and animal forms are universally present.
They will see the way weather conditions affect the environment. All this
will have been experienced as a result of using the viewfinder as a means
of visual stimulus.

The activity described above is one way of exploring the environment and it leads to consideration of purposeful use of the environment as a visual stimulus for drawing, painting and creative writing. Every classroom window is, in fact, a viewfinder framing a collection of associated coloured shapes, there for the taking, all different, all fascinating, all part of the child's immediate experience, if his attention is focused upon it.

Readings from creative prose and poetry can be used as starters for painting. The teacher will have his favourite poets. Choose examples which depend for their effect upon the generation of visual imagery. Gerard Manley Hopkins comes strongly to mind as a painter in words, for instance his 'The Starlight Night', from *Gerard Manley Hopkins* (W. H. Gardner), Penguin (London and Baltimore).

'Look at the stars! look, look up at the skies!
O look at all the fire-folk sitting in the air!
The bright boroughs, the circle-citadels there!
Down in dim woods the diamond delves! the elves-eyes!
The grey lawns cold where gold, where quick gold lies!
Wind-beat white-beam! airy abeles set on a flare!
Flake doves sent floating forth at a farmyard scare!
Ah well! it is all a purchase, all is a prize.'

The children do not, necessarily, have to understand every single nuance in order to arrive at the meaning of a poem. In any case perhaps the best way to understand Gerard Manley Hopkins is to paint him! Young children have an almost mystical power of transcription. To some the music of poetry is perhaps as pictorial as the word-painting. To quote an example from the opening of Dylan Thomas's *Under Milk Wood:*

It is Spring, moonless night in the small town, starless and bible-black, the cobble streets silent and the hunched, courters'-and-rabbits' wood limping invisible down to the sloeblack, slow, black, crowblack, fishingboat-bobbing sea.

I recall the boy who, having finished his art work, asked the teacher what he should do next. The teacher always kept a book of poems on his desk. He asked the boy if he had ever tried to illustrate a poem. 'No!' said the boy firmly. 'I don't like poetry.' The teacher mildly commented it wasn't necessary to like poetry in order to illustrate it. 'How about trying an experiment?' he suggested. The boy agreed unenthusiastically. He, like a good many lads at that stage of development, considered poetry to be 'cissy'. 'It's very simple,' said the teacher, 'I'll read a bit of a poem and if you hear words that make a picture come into your mind, stop me.' He opened a book of verses by John Betjeman at a poem called 'Parliament Hill Fields'. He read slowly in an even voice and when he spoke the words '. . . puffing sulphur to the sunset . . .,' relating to a goods train of old, the boy stopped him. 'Well,' said the teacher, 'describe what you can see.' The boy said, 'Round clouds of yellow against pink.' A few lines later the teacher read '. . . blackened girders . . .' and the boy ventured, 'black criss-crossing'. 'There you are, you see,' said the teacher in mild triumph, 'I said it was easy'. 'Yes,' agreed the boy, 'but I don't like poetry.'

The teacher remained unperturbed and was about to close the poetry book when a voice from across the room said, 'Sir, I've finished, I'd like to illustrate that poem.' The first boy bridled slightly. He did not like being ousted. Finally, both boys settled down and worked side by side. The paintings they produced were not remarkable but, towards the end of the period, the teacher overheard a quiet comment from the first boy to the second, 'Hey! it's *not bad*, is it? this poem?'

Whether that period should have been labelled English or art, whether the experience was poetry appreciation or creative art, is irrelevant. The teacher had used this technique deliberately and in a planned way. It may be that this boy found a new awareness of poetry, or words, or reading that day which might last throughout his life.

Movement as stimulus

The visual link between dance, movement and drawing, painting, modelling, is self-evident. The drawing in fig. 45 was produced by a 10-year-old girl. Carol had arrived at school in a new dirndle skirt and the teacher had asked her to make a series of continuous pirouettes across the classroom. This simple manœuvre focused the pupils attention on the short, intense and visually exciting skirt movement, and this provided powerful stimulus.

Dramatic stimulus

All of us from time to time encounter special experiences which consist in clear sharp images. Turning a corner to be confronted by a clutch of wood pigeons in a tall red hawthorn tree in full blossom and lit by brilliant golden evening sunlight (fig. 67).

Five London lads caught in a sudden squall of wind and rain make a frenzied dash for shelter under a tree then leap up into its lower branches.

John Kenway, senior lecturer in education, describes another such incident:

> On the beach at Marsden, Co. Durham, I found a twisted punctured piece of silvery looking sheet metal—almost certainly part of the fabric of a crashed aircfaft? When did it happen? Where was the rest of the plane? Just beyond the low water mark tantalisingly out of sight? What happened to the pilot? Did he escape? How? Would similar material, skilfully presented to the children, make them feel the need to 'tell someone'—to describe by writing or drawing or painting to communicate, to learn? What was the pilot's last radio message? How did he escape? What was he feeling?

Variation of routine is an effective stimulus. Change the environment from time to time, take them to the Zoo, to the local colliery, the docks, the woods, the railway station.

fig. 71   Zoo

Verbal stimulus

The spoken word can conjure up powerful visual images. Marion Richardson exploited this approach, which consisted of describing subject matter graphically and in detail, feeding visual information to the children by means of vivid word painting. Her book *Art and the Child*, University of London Press, describes her method in detail. It is a method which has much to recommend it and is of particular value in the area of visual imagination. Because it is specially relevant to art appreciation fuller details are given under 'The Fine Arts,' pages 102-107.

The reverse of the process is to present the child with a painting and invite him to write about it, or speak about it. The results are sometimes unexpected and often beautiful.

The poem below was written by Janet, aged 10, after seeing the painting *Three Brood Mares* by George Stubbs. It provides a good example of transcription of mood rather than of content:

fig. 72

The boy walked through the
unsettled meadow,
Where the horses were grazing,
And the restless still air
was blowing,
He felt dreamy and impressed,
He felt lonely, quiet and
timid
His mind was blured but
not realistic
His mind recovered,
And the light in the sky
fell
And he drifted away into
sleep.

It is possible to add considerably to the power of verbal stimulus if some of the concepts can be linked with direct visual stimulus. In the case of the pigeons, for instance, a stuffed or real bird in the classroom would be a great help; as would a tree if one could be seen from the classroom window.

But perhaps the most persuasive stimulus is the use of leading questions. The function of leading questions in our context is to motivate the pupil to gather visual information in a form in which he can use it in the work he is doing. The leading question may have many answers; an answer from one child will differ from that of another. The sensitive teacher using leading questions will not expect a given answer, or the same answer. He will see the leading question as providing the child with a visual problem to solve, or at least to analyse, in an open-ended and personal way.

Suppose the theme is 'Shape' and the work in progress a drawing; a portrait of a friend (see fig. 40). Leading questions could be framed as follows:

1 Can you see the shape his hair makes?
2 Can you point to the lines which make the outline of his hair shape?
3 Can you think of a word which describes how his hair looks?
4 Would you say his hair is light, medium or dark?
5 Can you point to the line which makes the shape of his face?
6 Look at the distance between the top of his head and his chin; how far down are his eyes, his ears, his mouth?
7 How many colours can you see in his eyes?
8 What holds his head up?
9 Can you point to the lines which make the neck shape?
10 What comes next below his neck?
11 What sort of stuff is his shirt made of . . . can you give me six adjectives which describe it?
12 If you look past him, what can you see?

If the theme is 'shape' and the work in hand is a painting of 'the school' the leading questions could be slanted to help the pupil to recognise the component shapes in the subject in much the same way as the portrait drawing, but now there might be a greater variety of colour.

1 Is the wall a pure colour?
2 How would you describe it?
3 Is it the same colour all over?
4 Which is the lightest colour you can see?
5 Which is the biggest shape?
6 Is it just one big shape by itself or does it contain smaller shapes as well?
7 What are they?

Exactly the same type of questions can be asked about groups of objects set up for the children to look at, or for the single unusual object imported into the classroom. The teacher will readily devise appropriate leading questions. The answers to them will indicate to the teacher what degree of penetration the child is bringing to his looking. In other words whether he is merely looking, or really seeing.

Change as stimulus

A change of medium, from paint to pastel, or charcoal, or felt-tip pen, or ball-point pen, or acrylic paint, from time to time is essential and children should be encouraged to experiment. A new medium is always a stimulus. If the group have been working for any length of time on painting, a change of basic skill, as well as of medium, may well act as a vital stimulus. Screen printing, pattern-making by tie and dye, print-making using various types of block, resist techniques, are all basic skills and they all have a particular flavour and fascination. Pupils are curious about new processes. The motivating power of curiosity is considerable. A number of these basic skills are dealt with on pages 112 to 140. References are given to books dealing with them for teachers who would like to read more about them. Basic skills of drawing, painting, print-making, modelling, carving, relief, collage, appliqué, embroidery and so on are the equivalent, in art, to spelling, vocabulary, handwriting, grammar, syntax in creative writing. The basic skills of the verbal arts must be learned before creative English writing can be achieved. We must be sure that children are in possession of the art basic skills if we expect them to produce creative expression in any of the art forms.

Materials can stimulate. They can also dominate. Modern materials and media such as plastics, perspex, polystyrene, acrylic paints, oil pastels, and the proprietary craft materials all have their uses and attractions, but one must remember that they are only vehicles of expression not forms of expression in themselves. There is a great vogue at the moment for using waste materials, plastic containers, old packages, packing papers, egg boxes, toilet-roll centres, milk-bottle tops, drinking straws, spatulas, sweet wrappings. Many of these are useful and in some cases invaluable, but remember that an egg box by any other name is still an egg box.

Remedial stimulus

Figs. 73 and 74 are linked. They are both by the same so-called 'backward' girl in a normal junior school in England. They represent two essays, one in writing, and one in painting. The same visual stimulus, a stuffed fish in a glass case, was provided for both. The same teacher introduced both activities with similar discussions. Both were done in the same room. Only the medium was different. The age of the girl was 9 years.

The writing, as can be seen, is a few jumbled letters of unreadable and meaningless hieroglyph. It was the best the girl could do. The painting is clear, eloquent, expressive and meaningful.

If as educators we accept that it is our function to evaluate how much a child can absorb, and what is his power and quality of expression, which of these two pieces of work should we accept as evidence?

fig. 73   Fish, girl aged 9 years

The sequence of events which is described below would not seem unusual in many schools today; but it was ahead of its time in 1957.

On the first day of term in September of that year a group of about twenty 'backward' junior girls, Class Three, were waiting for their new teacher. They had had a long series of supply teachers and this, added to their low ability, had diminished their interest in school and their confidence in themselves.

The headmistress, a far-sighted woman, had decided to tackle the problem of these 'slow-learners' by appointing a qualified art teacher who, it was hoped, would use creative art activities as the point of contact. An able, and suitable, teacher was available at the time.

At the end of the first week Class Three's room was decorated with the children's colourful paintings. The impact of the work was strong and attracted the attention of the girls in the 'academic' class next door. One of them said, within earshot, 'Look at all those *smashing* paintings.' Such praise was a new experience for Class Three.

By half-term a full-sized barrow-boy's barrow was added to the paintings. It was constructed in a corner of their room. They stocked it with papier-mâché marrows (squash), oranges, apples, potatoes, rhubarb, all painted and given price tickets. A patterned awning was made for the top and fixed in place. They made cardboard money and with it, as maths, they shopped for papier-mâché produce. Members of the staff came to see what was going on.

fig. 74

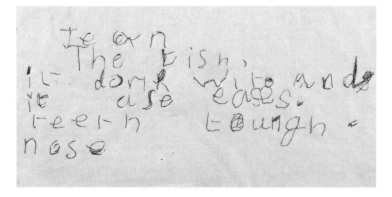

The effect of the success of the project upon Class Three was very marked. For the first time their work had been approved by other children and by other teachers. They became animated and enthusiastic.

Other rewarding sessions followed. History took the form amongst other things of making paper models of Queen Elizabeth 1st. They made string fishes, paper weavings, twig dolls, large paper hats, five-foot paper angels for Christmas decorations. Class Three's room became a centre of visual interest for the whole school, and for school inspectors and other visitors.

The experiment of approaching these children through creative art and craft had been successful. The new feeling of confidence which the children had acquired supported them when they tackled other activities.

Linda and Barbara for instance both went forward two and a half years in reading age after the first six months.

The above account is factual. The art stimulus did much more than involve the children in art activity. It proved to be of significant remedial, and educational, value to them. The fish and lettering in figs. 73 and 74 are by one of these girls.

Every teacher, at some time in his career, is likely to be faced with the problem of backwardness. I am speaking not of the educationally sub-normal child in the 'special' school but of retardation in the normal school. Innumerable cases can be cited of the remedial effect of success in art, of children being 'motivated' by the excitement of painting, drawing or craft work when all else had failed.

It is, beyond doubt, a fact that whether he be backward or brilliant or just average, the junior school child is capable of producing art work of a remarkably high standard, but he may not do so if he thinks the teacher is prepared to accept anything less than the best. Every subtle device the teacher can invent should be used to cajole, persuade, flatter, goad, decoy, prompt, tempt, dare, provoke, encourage the child to work to the best of his ability.

9 Environment

If the reader will think back over the ground covered so far, it will be realised that the most significant work discussed has been that which has resulted from study and analysis of the environment. The *Autumn Frieze* was rooted in the environment of the school. Most of the 'project headings' are environmental in character. Decoration, for example, is manifestly environmental. Man modifies his environment by decorating it, with results which vary between the magnificent and the aesthetically totally unacceptable.

A major function of the education service is to help the child to adjust to his environment; to enjoy it, to develop within him the ability to discriminate about the quality of his environment. It is the responsibility of the education service to provide the child with a wholesome school environment appropriate to his needs as a developing human being. The context in which we are thinking is of the total environment, social, emotional, but with special reference to the physical and visual aspects.

In order to know, one must explore. If one is to come to terms with one's environment one must, amongst other things, explore it visually. To do this effectively one must use as many as possible of the available aids to seeing. We have already considered the viewfinder and its uses. What are the other available aids?

All junior schools should possess, or have access to, a camera. There is a good choice these days, of modestly priced, single-lens reflex cameras which enable the photographer to carry out a wide range of work. There are few school common-rooms which do not include a keen photographer. Children can quickly learn to operate quite complex instruments and in doing so a valuable link can be established with geometry, optics, engineering. If finance will not permit the type of camera mentioned above a great deal can be done with a quite inexpensive one. The main difference would be that close-up photography would be less possible.

Photography provides two spheres of activity:
(1) The making of slide photographs for projection
(2) The production of negatives from which prints can be made.

If these capabilities are linked to problem-solving situations the pupils will be involved in visual exploration and the development of a sense of values in much the same way as the boys who took part in the *Autumn Frieze* project, and a sense of involvement with the environment will grow.

Suppose a theme were mooted for instance on 'Textures'. Suppose you have a group of 10- or 11-year-old children who have learned to focus the camera and set the appropriate aperture. If they find the light-meter difficult to understand and operate the teacher could help with this. Then let each pupil take, say, two shots at any two textured surfaces which he has found and which specially interests him or her. The photographic project could be the culmination of a series of explorations of textures in other media. A colour film is not very expensive, once in a while. After every member of the group has pressed the button twice the film is rolled back, packed up and sent away to be processed. When it comes back the class will assemble in the blacked-out classroom, every member agog to see his or her own photograph appear on the screen. This situation, appropriately handled, results in intense excitement and anticipation. No normal child can fail to come out of this situation visually stimulated and more visually aware of some aspects of his surroundings.

If the film used was black and white the prints can be laid on the table for comment and appraisal. Later, perhaps, a montage might be put together.

The camera is not indispensable. A great deal of work can be done without a camera and at very little cost. Slides, for instance, can be made from scrap materials without the use of a camera. Most amateur photographers have a stock of unsuccessful colour transparencies. The plastic frames from these (fig. 2) can be used in school (the reader is referred back to page 17). Using wide transparent sticky tape, stick a square over one face. Place the 'subject' on the sticky side. Then stick a second square of sticky tape over the other face of the plastic slide frame. You now have the subject sandwiched between two layers of transparent sticky tape, and supported by the plastic frame. This may now be used in the standard 35-mm projector. Good 'subjects' to start with are granular substances like salt, sugar. A few grains of sand when projected look like large circular translucent pebbles. Magnification is very great; as many as ten thousand times. In some ways this device is an improvement on the microscope. There is no problem of manipulation and focusing; and the children can view as a group and so share the, to them, miraculous visual experience of having revealed, large before their eyes, aspects of their environment of which they were only dimly aware before.

As soon as the children grasp this procedure they will search for, find and invent all kinds of substances to use. The activity stimulates, and makes use of, the child's inborn curiosity about his environment, and especially the minute things in it. Slide frames may be cut from cardboard if redundant plastic frames are not available.

For the junior school which can rig up an improvised 'darkroom' light-sensitive photographic paper provides many possibilities. If a sheet of sensitised paper is laid flat down in very weak light and two or three objects of clearly defined shape are arranged on its surface, and left for a few moments, and if the paper is then placed in a solution of paper developer and 'fixed' in hypo, the white silhouette of the leaves, or ferns, or keys, or scissors, or whatever may have been placed there, appears. Once again, when the pupils grasp the principle, they will show great inventiveness in finding and using all kinds of materials and specimens in the production of such photographs and in the finding will explore and analyse and discriminate in terms of the environment.

Drawing and painting may be used in the same way as the camera, to stimulate an exploratory approach to environment.

The *Autumn Frieze* project involved the pupils in a series of close observations of their familiar school environment; it evoked new awareness of environment, it called for judgement about environment. All of this was foreseen by the teacher, before the work began, as likely to happen

fig. 75   House, by Japanese boy aged 11

and likely to be of educational value to the boys.

The Van Gogh reed pen drawing provoked systematic searching for certain kinds of plants, in the town environment of that particular school. It was a 'starter' of environmental exploration, and revealed many plants never suspected of being in the locale.

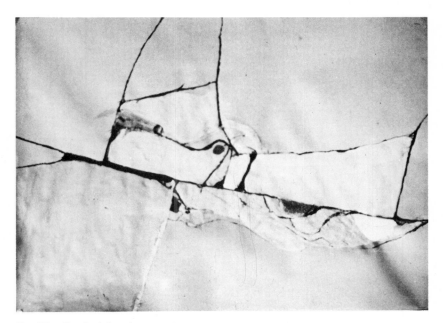

fig. 76   Cracked flagstones

Children are naturally inquisitive and acquisitive. If your school is near a beach, walk them from end to end of it and see what they collect en-route—driftwood, pebbles, feathers, corks, wreckage, sea-plants, shells, eroded forms.

The countryside, the woodland, the quarry, the gravel pit, the seaside, all provide differing and characteristic material.

If they live in town let them collect drawings of:

Town chimneys; tracings of lettering from posters and street notices; patterns from railings; architectural features; rubbings from manhole covers; photographs of crowds; skylines, reflections, silhouettes, studies of lamp posts, pillar boxes, slot machines.

To walk along the beach, in the country or the town or suburban equivalent, is valid as an art lesson.

Encourage the children to use sketch-books.

Select individual items in the immediate vicinity of the school and set visual problems to be solved. Fig. 76 shows a typical study, in this case of cracked flagstones. Take single trees, an abandoned car, a house, single growing plants. Make a collection of drawings of single windows of as many different kinds as possible.

The previous two or three pages have indicated some ways of using art media and skills to awaken and develop the child's reaction to the physical world in which he lives. They have also hinted at the sort of art activities which can be initiated by direct observation of, and curiosity about, the school buildings and their immediate surroundings.

Let us now go on to examine another, more immediate, aspect of the school milieu.

fig. 77a   fig. 77b

The classroom environment

The school interior reflects the personalities of the boys, girls and teachers who spend so much of their time there, and the sort of activities which go on in it. The atmosphere of every room is a product of the interests and activities of pupils and teacher, but probably above everything else it is dependent upon the sensitivity of the teacher. A lively visual sense is immediately apparent. The over-fastidious attitude is as obvious as the 'couldn't-care-less' approach. In this affluent society there are still many deprived children who come from inadequate homes. Their school may be all they will ever experience of decent living conditions while they are growing up. The responsible teacher will want to give every child in his care the best possible setting in which to grow.

The most potent visual factor in any interior is the quality of display. Ill-placed, badly hung, disproportionate or badly framed pictures will destroy visual harmony. In the commercial world those shops which are most attractive are made so by distinguished display and subtle interior decor. In some respects the school is a cross between home and shop. It is a place where children live a substantial part of their early lives and in which there are tempting collections of educational materials, and walls hung with pictures, and other forms of display. The presentation of pictures, whether they are produced by professional artists or by the children themselves, and of collections of teaching materials, if it is to achieve an acceptable standard of display must be carried out with care and a regard for visual harmony and amenity. Display should aim at enlivening the interior, attracting the attention of the viewer, and helping in the cross-fertilisation of ideas. To be effective it need not be elaborate but it must be trim and clean. Dusty or paint-splattered display boards should be papered over or, better still, painted. Corners of art work or pictures should not be allowed to hang loose. Dressmakers' pins are better to fasten up work than drawing pins. The heads of drawing pins are too large and visually aggressive. Repaint old shelving (fig. 77a).

A staple gun is quicker and more effective than either pins or drawing pins. Eccentric placing or bilateral symmetry does not help. Simple placing (fig. 77b) is more effective.

Highly coloured wide mounts militate against colour harmony. Narrow mounts of neutral colour, grey, buff, black, white, are more economical of space and less obtrusive. Practise discipline and restraint in display.

'This week's colour is purple.' One often sees visually exciting collections of objects all of one colour shown against a ground of the same colour. Well carried out this can be valuable experience of colour. If you go to the trouble of setting up a 'yellow corner' or a 'green wall', don't just look at it. Use it as subject material for painting.

The principles of good display do not only apply to paintings but to everything which is 'put on show'. If, in addition to day-to-day fare, exceptional objects and materials are brought in as stimulus, do not waste half their impact by leaving them lying around—display them. They will attract more attention. If 'pattern' is the educational point, and a display is projected, let it be set up in a patterned style.

The texture table with its shells and tree-bark and frosted glass and wire-mesh and netting and so on is put there for children to look at and to handle. Display them; or let the children display them on a suitable ground. Even though they are bound to be moved around as the children pick them up and examine them, begin with them set out in a dignified and thought-out arrangement. Most children enjoy arranging things. There will be no shortage of volunteers to keep watch on your display, to put the objects back in your original placing and, in so doing, a liking, and perhaps a facility, for display may be aquired.

A good classroom environment is one which by its contents provokes the children's curiosity. The texture corner has been mentioned. The boys will quickly furnish a machinery display with bits of old bicycle, clocks (fig. 79), electrics, radio, television, motorcar parts, cog wheels, and so on. The potent fascination of the strange and the unfamiliar can be roused by a 'curiosity' table. Who could resist a glass eye, an antique egg-timer . . . a pair of crimping irons . . . a glass prism . . . a Radiometer . . . a crystal garden . . . a dried sea-horse . . . a stethoscope . . . a chunk of rock crystal . . . an ammonite . . . a gourd . . . an old mandoline . . . a stopwatch . . . a sea urchin . . .? Display, which evokes fascination, will provide germs of ideas for creative expression of all kinds.

Many schools make use of floral decorations and of indoor plants. A vase of fresh flowers can do much to enliven a drab interior. Remember to remove them when they fade!

Lack of storage accommodation is frequently the cause of difficulty.

fig. 78 Texture table

fig. 79 Mechanical objects

Untidy piles of last week's or last month's art work do nothing to improve the interior. Some of the work has to be kept. Store what you can out of sight. Any you cannot store put on display. That which cannot be either stored or displayed must be stacked economically and tidily if chaos is to be avoided. A chaotic environment is not normally conducive to creative work and thinking.

Children's art work well presented can be a potent factor in creating a vibrant and colourful school environment.

10 Revolution and variation

'Education is not filling a pot, it is lighting a fire,' said Sir Alec Clegg, Education Officer, West Riding of Yorkshire. His aphorism epitomises the revolution which has been taking place in educational thinking and practice in the last forty years or so. The change has been a move away from hammering in the 3 Rs and towards a realisation of the nature of learning by experience; towards a redefinition of education.

By education in the context of the junior school we mean the development and growth of the child, physically, mentally, socially and emotionally. We mean growth in personality through experience; a process of self-fulfilment achieved by the child for himself, by exploration, by self-discovery, by self-involvement, in emotional, intellectual and sensual experiences. It has been said that 'education is experience made significant'. It is in the area of experience that we can draw from art and craft the maximum educational benefit for the child. This is change; and the change is still taking place; as is research into what changes are still necessary. The curriculum research centres in the United States, and elsewhere, and the Schools Council in Britain are working towards the same end. In particular, at the moment, the Schools Council is funding research into Primary Education in general through a project based on Lancaster University. It is also supporting a project based on Goldsmiths College, London, which is to look at the present position and future possibilities of art and craft for the 8–13-year-old middle school children. To quote from the introductory leaflet of the Goldsmith Project:

> . . . some people see the value of Art and Craft as heightening visual, tactile and spatial awareness. Others emphasize its significance in problem solving and enquiry.
> Others are concerned especially with fulfilling the imaginative and expressive potential of the individual. And yet others wish to develop a feeling for its contribution to the quality of life of the community. These are interlocking activities.

Of the total problem of teaching art and craft in junior schools the Goldsmith introduction says:

> 'There is no one, overall, way, nor any solution which can apply generally. The experience of each child, each teacher and each school grows within the possibilities and limitations of each particular set of circumstances.'

The last three lines above are another way of saying that conditions vary from school to school. With this every junior-school teacher will agree.

Teachers know that adaptability is the essential quality for any member of the profession. When they move from one school to another, or when a new member of the staff arrives, they know that adjustment will be called for. But what are the main ways in which conditions vary; what are the differences between one school and another. Are they significant?

Variations in accommodation

The overall situation at any given time and place is likely to resemble the curate's egg; good in parts, dubious in some places and bad in others. Accommodation, and the way it is used, will vary from complete freedom and open doors on the one hand to, on the other, rigid compartmentalisation into separate classrooms in schools where pockets of reaction still linger. Some authorities, with attitudes halfway between, provide specially equipped art rooms. In such cases the art impact within the school can be considerable, especially if the art work produced there is deployed about the school. The advantage of the special art room is that it makes art and craft immediately available, with everything to hand; providing all who use it observe basic studio drill, tidiness and cleanliness. Generally speaking the special art studios are used by all the general teachers. If there is an art-trained teacher on the staff he or she acts as a general teacher but makes his/her special knowledge available to the staff generally.

Some junior schools in the Inner London Education Authority have special studios manned by specialist art teachers. In one such, individual children or small groups, as well as painting in their own rooms, may detach at any time from their normal routine and may go to the studio to work if they need more than the basic equipment provided in their classrooms. The standard of children's art in that school is high. It is a major visual amenity and covers walls round the school with vigorous and colourful work.

It is possible that the provision of special art studios could lead to art and craft becoming isolated and separated out from other school activities, but this is unlikely to happen where it is the school's custom to give creative work its true place and to exhibit it about the school.

The example given above is a case of an extra teacher additional to the normal staff and used as a specialist. This is a luxury not always possible administratively or financially. There is undoubtedly a place for the art specialist in the junior school, but *not* to teach *only* art. The need is for art specialists with junior teacher training to teach general subjects, to be a normal member of the teaching team but at the same time to be able to act in an advisory capacity within the school in their own special subject, i.e. art. The provision of a teacher with appropriate art training is probably more important than the provision of a special studio, though it is beyond question that a room set apart for art and craft is a valuable incentive to art activity.

Any teacher, reading the above comments, who is one of that too large percentage with conditions nothing like as good as those described, may be forgiven a sardonic smile when she recalls the exhaustion and the frustration of attempting to provide art and craft for 40 children in under-sized classrooms, ordinary desks, and water carried by bucket from the far end of the corridor. The only possible solution in these cases is to grit one's teeth, to contrive and make do and to resolve, for the sake of the children, not to give up hope. The problem can be minimised somewhat if painting groups are kept small and work to a rota. Organisation can be made easier

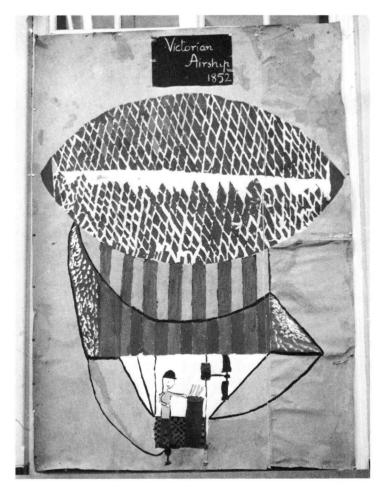

fig. 80 Victorian balloon—large-scale display

if groups of helpers are trained to do specific jobs, i.e. fetch water, give out brushes, collect paints. There is no law that says all children must work big; occasional work on a small scale has value. It is important, however, to enable children who *want* to, to paint large. Leave a space vacant on the display board and fasten paper to that and let them paint there. Use the wall to fasten the paper to with some malleable gum adhesive (U.K.: Plastic-tak) if there is no display board. Use the floor, spread out into the corridor, or the assembly hall. It is possible to overcome poor conditions by pre-planning. Good amenities do not guarantee good art, but they help. Bad conditions do not necessarily mean bad art; more often than not they act as a spur to invention. Some of the finest art work is to be seen in adverse school conditions where to produce art at all is little short of miraculous.

An ancient school building which comes to mind is constructed as a rectangular hall with classrooms all round. The hall is used as a multi-purpose centre and is served by a team of teachers. Large-scale art work takes place in the hall (fig. 80), and smaller-scale work in the classrooms. A part-time specialist art teacher teaches there and at least part of his duty is to supply art and craft 'know-how' to his less specialised colleagues.

This works well in this school because there is a friendly team spirit in this group of teachers.

The biggest discrepancy in accommodation is between the new open-plan buildings, with their purpose-built amenity and multi-purpose activity areas, and the many ancient buildings which will be with us for many years yet. Even so, flexibility of approach and method can greatly reduce the wide divergencies. Begin by leaving classroom doors open. Continue by persuading your Authority to knock doorways through party walls.

Variations in equipment

Another variable factor is the type of furniture and equipment. The ordinary standard classroom single desk is hopelessly inadequate for art work. At least two or three flat formica-topped dual tables are indispensable in every room or art and craft area. So too are two or three simple easels. The Inner London Education Authority at one time provided special easels (U.K. Mansard Units fig. 81), which provided a large stable painting surface. Two of these placed side by side produce enough room for a large group work.

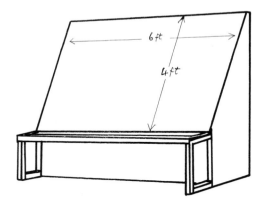

fig. 81   Mansard easel

No good head teacher will ever refuse requests for materials until the school funds are exhausted; but start from a position of strength. When the children produce something interesting go along and say, 'Look what we've done. We could have done much better if we had more to do it with!'

Never be afraid to ask for the materials you need.

The good teacher will be effective in any conditions, but appropriate materials, equipment and accommodation will add to the efficiency of even the best teacher. Every teacher should expect to be provided with adequate facilities.

Other variants are, the social structure of the neighbourhood, the catchment area from which the pupils come, the differing degree of ability in the children, composition of the staff, and philosophy of the head teacher. Perhaps the most vital factors affecting the individual teacher are the ethos of the school: the teaching policy, the approach and method advocated by the head and how it is organised.

Every teacher in the end must decide on his own approach; between rigidity and freedom, between compartmentalisation and 'open-door'; between the traditional and known, and the experimental and new. The highest single priority is for the teacher to be adaptable.

Junior school children find total freedom difficult to deal with, and this is especially so in art and craft at the 9–10–11-year stage. They need the challenge of a problem-solving situation, or the support of a learned skill. The halfway line between total freedom and regimentation may well be the teacher-structured, teacher-selected, situation calculated beforehand to lead to known results; the setting of the same problem to all the pupils and allowing them total freedom to solve the problem in their own personal way, and expecting as many different solutions as there are children; and the corollary, teaching them all the same basic skill, e.g. tie-dyeing, and expecting as many different uses of that skill as there are different children.

In some schools the teacher will find himself part of a 'team-teaching' group. Other schools may have an art specialist on the staff. Most schools will have no specialist. Make the most of any help you can get from any art specialists you may encounter.

Because of the variety of situations in schools the teacher, as has been said before, must be prepared to make adjustments. This calls for a mature outlook, understanding, perceptiveness and sensitivity.

Of the qualities which go to make a good teacher I would place sensitivity very high, if not top of the list. The teacher must be sensitive to atmosphere, to the quality of the environment, and, perhaps the most unpredictable variant of them all, to the reactions of the children, their problems, moods, ideals, and fears, to their aesthetic attitudes and particularly their standards. The teacher must be sensitive to the teaching climate in the school, whether it is positive or negative or neutral, and must find a way to make a constructive contribution within that context.

11 The fine arts

Children should at least have heard of the Renaissance painters and the French Impressionists before they leave junior school. Most of them see something of prehistoric painting and hear through the popular media of extremists riding bicycles through paint and then across canvases. It should be possible also to interest them in Leonardo da Vinci's sketchbooks and Van Gogh's ear and so to fill in a little of the gap between the Cave Artists and the Action Painters.

The enterprising teacher will use: TV programmes, reproductions, films, slides, visits to galleries, to exhibitions, original works of art, and the school library, to set the artist's work before the pupils. The B.B.C. Radio Vision Service is also a valuable aid.

Earlier in this book an example was given of the use of the school library, in this context. The reader will perhaps recall the little girl who went to the library to fetch the Van Gogh book. She was fortunate. The shelves of her school library were well stocked with monographs on the famous artists, and omnibus volumes dealing with famous collections. They were the standard publications, not books of pictures, thought by well-meaning but misguided adults to be 'suitable for children'. A good policy when stocking the school library is to provide as wide a variety as possible of biographical studies of individual artists with a preference for those series providing the maximum number of illustrations. There are many such series, modestly priced and acceptable in quality. The little girl and the Van Gogh reed pen incident illustrates the sort of use to which the library can be put. It also gives a good example of one of the best ways to approach 'art appreciation' with young children. In that case they became vitally involved with how Van Gogh worked because they identified with him by using his medium, the reed pen. They then compared *their* results with his results, and showed real understanding of his work. The most telling method of art appreciation at any educational level is that of practical involvement.

Another method of invoking deep personal involvement is for the teacher to select a well-known painting which is not too intricate in content and one which the children have not seen before. The teacher then describes the picture in minute detail and accuracy without first showing the picture to the children. He then invites the painting group to paint it piece by piece, shape by shape as each bit is described. There is an element of game about this procedure. The children have the problem of visualising the forms. The teacher has the challenge of exact description and in the end the 'pay-off' comes in terms of anticipation of the exciting moment when the teacher reveals the original. The comparison of theirs with the professional product produces searching scrutiny of the original or the reproduction of the original. This is a valid activity on grounds of descriptive language, memory training, the stimulation of visual imagery, colour description, colour mixing, appreciation of the art of the master painter. (Rousseau would be a good subject.) The practice is suggested in the context of art appreciation, to be tried perhaps once or at the most twice, and not as a procedure for normal art activity (fig. 82).

Reproductions of works of art are a mixed blessing with the balance

fig. 82   Henri Rousseau, Portrait of
Pierre Loti, 1891, Kunsthaus, Zurich

on the credit side. No school interior these days need be without some manifestation of fine art. Cost is no longer an obstacle.

At the same time, along with exposure to reproductions, the 7- to 11-year-old children should be given the chance to see original art in order to keep their sense of values straight. The best educational experience is significant first-hand experience. Yet because of the mass media today's children are constantly fed with a diet of second-hand experience. The effect of an original work of art cannot be adequately transmitted by small coloured reproductions any more than Beethoven's Choral Symphony can be adequately experienced through a hole in a wooden box, or two holes in two boxes, in spite of the vast technical advances which are today being made in high-fidelity sound reproduction.

Most schools and education authorities recognise this fact, and the schools arrange visits to galleries and exhibitions so that children may see original works of art. Education authorities provide transport, or finance for transport, and in many cases they also provide loan services of original works of art and craft for display in schools.

The London County Council, now the Greater London Council, instituted and operated a Patronage of the Arts scheme which provided for the setting aside of a sum of public money each year for the purchase and commissioning of works of art. These were then sited in public places, frequently in association with architectural projects. Schools were beneficiaries under this scheme and one recalls numerous examples; the Mary Fedden mural which still enhances the lives of the London East End Girls' School; the mosaic in the primary school in Chelsea designed by Francis Carr and constructed from every imaginable different type of minutiae which could serve as tesserae, bits of mirror, Victorian tiles, pebbles, shells, all set at the child's eye level so that the boys and girls can explore the surface with eyes and fingers; the whole work producing a magical and enriching effect upon the school interior.

figs. 83a, b   Francis Carr mosaic

Another example is the sculptor who was commissioned to provide a figure for the school grounds and who visited the school with his *maquette* and discussed with the children the work he proposed to make. He was so impressed by their comments that he modified his design. Such a good relationship developed between children and artist that he invited them to visit his studio and some of them actually helped him with the final stages of the work.

Fig. 84 shows the work of another sculptor, Ralph Brown, sited in the grounds of a school in South London.

Every artist who takes his easel out into town or country to work knows of the fascinated curiosity with which onlookers view what he is doing. This is seen at its extreme in children. Witness the crowds round the sign-writer at work, the unfortunate motorist changing a wheel. This is a fertile vein for teaching as yet hardly tapped. Why not, as a colleague suggested, offer the potter, the sculptor, the painter room to work in the junior school and let the children stand round and watch and absorb and ask questions, and wonder and experience and be enthused. There would be a rich field for co-operation between schools and Colleges of Art, and Colleges of Education Art Departments. Advanced students could very well work at their chosen craft in schools with great advantage to all concerned. The school might commission a work, or buy a work. What better aim for a 'bring and buy' or jumble sale than to amass £50 to buy a picture for the school. Imagine going, with money in the teacher's pocket, with a group of children, to choose a picture from the local gallery or dealer or exhibition. That would provide an experience no child who took part in it would ever forget. Better still plan a trip to London, see the sights and buy a picture at the same time.

The Society for Education through Art, in Britain, has for the last

fig. 84   St Christopher, by Ralph Brown

twenty-one years organised an annual exhibition called 'Pictures for Schools'. Distinguished contemporary artists are invited to submit work and in addition contributions are drawn widely from other leading painters, sculptors, graphic artists, embroiderers. There is no question of this being an exhibition of pictures painted specially for children. The criterion for the selectors is the best work, in any genre, at a price education authorities are able to afford. The purchasers come from educational institutions all over the country and sales amounted to about £7,000 in 1969. This exhibition, the brain-child of Nan Youngman, is now established as an annual event in the education world of Britain. The purchasers have confidence. They know they can buy and will get good value in educational terms. Many Local Education Authority art collections bought their first works from 'Pictures for Schools', while many use it as a main source of supply. Many schools and many children have reason to be grateful to S.E.A., to Nan Youngman and to her teams of workers.

   Added value can be drawn from visits to galleries and exhibitions by two simple techniques. The first is to provide each child with a modest typed/duplicated questionnaire before they set out. The questions should be tailored according to the age of the children and would be structured, basically, to require close looking at the pictures in order to give an answer. The questions could be such as: how many 'modern' pictures are there? How many sad pictures? Write down the title of the picture which you like best. Why do you like that one? Can you tell which is the oldest picture in the gallery? Why do you think it is old? Can you find a picture which tells you about history? or another which tells you about geography? Write down what it is which tells you about the history or geography. Can you find a picture about weather? Look at picture number X; describe it.

   The second of these techniques is to ask the children to write about one

special picture when they return to school; or about a picture of their
choice. The following quotations are from primary childrens' writings and
sayings about pictures and other works of art.

'We saw sculptures of people lying down with tunnels through them.'
Entry in her diary by a 7-year-old girl, referring to a reclining figure
by Henry Moore which she had seen while on a school visit to the Tate
Gallery, London.
Overheard at an exhibition; a lad of 8 or 9 looking at a large modern
sculpture, 'Dad! did he do it on purpose?'
A 7-year-old child was taken to see an open-air exhibition of sculpture in Holland Park in London. He stopped in front of a large
abstract metal sculpture which had on it a heavy patina of red iron
oxide rust. 'Did they dig it up?' he asked.

These quotations are not intended as comment on modern abstract art!
They are quoted to show the intensity of the child's reaction, and his
unexpected turn of mind when he is confronted by the unfamiliar.

Sometimes the child's reaction to the work of art can be channelled by
the sensitive teacher into creative prose, or poetry, writing. Conversely, the
child's creative writings about works of art are an indication, sometimes
the only indication, of the nature of his reaction to the work of art. The
following are two examples of creative writing triggered off by looking at
some of the pictures just arrived in the school as part of the circulating
picture scheme.

The first, by Fiona, age 10, was written after looking at *The Thames at
Twickenham* by Richard Wilson.

'The River' by Fiona Harris

The leafy gold that covered the trees, plopped into the restless water,
the stones showed blurred, on the bottom.
The gurgling water poured down,
Away from village or town,
And as it poured through the deserted wood,
The leaves fell down as if they could,
Spend the longest time in the air,
But who would care? who would care?
For this unsettled, restless sport?
Nobody, nobody, nobody, no naught!

The leaves fall down and form a splash,
Some animal heard the old gate clash,
Hark! away a squirrel flees!
Everything's quiet but the bees,
The Wind must have banged the gate,
The dreamy woodland's free of hate,
Once more, once more, that country scene,
Is as it was, as it has been.

The second is by Elizabeth after looking at a Chagall painting.

'Mad Cow' by Elizabeth, age 10

A blundering lively cow shoots up into the air which is a rusty colour,
frolicking madly as he goes all the other cows murmur oh go fall in
the hay leaping swiftly over both stones and haze. Muffled cows in
the background on the dusty plain.
Energetic is he that rises soaring into the sky. Maybe from the
dirty dusty road comes the tired old wandrer and will slay those in the
way.

When selecting pictures to hang around the school it may not be a bad
criterion to choose those which might be the best stimuli to creative writing.

Children like what they like. At this stage the word taste means nothing
to them. My first memory of deriving pleasure and aesthetic experience
directly from a work of art is of a garish version of Turner's *Ulysses
deriding Polyphemus,* printed by transfer on the 10×8 in lid of a tin of
biscuits which was given to my family as a Christmas gift. I was 8 years
old at the time. We were not well endowed with worldly goods. This was the
first work of art I had seen. I was spellbound by the title, but most of all
by the hot browns, reds and oranges. I have always responded most readily
to warm colour. Some considerable time later I was shown a much more
accurate print of the same picture, on paper. I was astonished by the difference. I preferred the crude hot version on the biscuit tin. How would
you like to see a *real* painting by Turner? I was asked. I was thrilled at
the prospect; but what I saw was one of his early topographical works. I
was vastly disappointed. I had expected to see a magical, mystical, atmospheric harmony of golden yellows and I saw what to me, then, was a dull
photographic landscape. But I was captivated by this artist who could
paint in two different styles. The Tate Gallery in London is the place to see
Turners. Books about Turner served in the interim but a visit to London
to see Turner's pictures remained a dream and an ambition for years. I
have never lost my love and respect for Turner. It started with a crude, in-
accurate print on a biscuit tin. We must strive to provide the very best we
can for the pupils, but as can be seen above, even a fifth-rate reproduction
can strike a spark which will remain alive indefinitely.

A teacher played a record of the storm music from Wagner's *The Flying
Dutchman.* He then showed the children four pictures: a Sisley spring
landscape, a Cézanne village street, a Ruisdael landscape in a storm, and
Turner's *Cottage in the Cornfield.* He invited the children to say which
picture looked like the music sounded. There was an almost unanimous
vote for the Ruisdael. Later in the English lesson they saw a parallel
between the Flying Dutchman, the Ruisdael and the Witches' scene from
Macbeth.

Children react positively if somewhat unpredictably to the work of the
professional artist whether he be the most *avant garde* contemporary painter
or an old master. Fine art plays such an important role in the environment
that education must take account of it by ensuring that it forms part of the
child's experience in the junior school.

12 The teacher

Initial training

The special problem in art in the upper junior school in Britain at any rate would appear to stem from the fact that the average junior school teacher (I do not include students who take art as a main subject at college), as produced by the present system, receives insufficient training and background in art and craft to feel confidence in himself and his ability to involve the children in significant art and craft activity. More 'specialist' teaching at upper junior level (9, 10, 11 years) is required, and it seems that 'team-teaching' holds out the best hope of meeting this need, and the best method of applying it. If each 'team of teachers' were to include one specialist art teacher or at least one able ex-student with Main Art in his/her armoury, who is keen on the subject and who would make his knowledge and advice available to his other colleagues, this would 'leaven the loaf', and make art expertise available to a wider range of children in the 8 to 11 range than at present.

For 'team-teaching' to become general education authorities must be persuaded of the need for reorganisation, especially in regard to appointment and allocation of staff, and they must be prepared to make the administrative changes to bring about such reorganization.

The special problem in art

As a broad generalization the 'water-shed' between 'infant' and 'junior' occurs at about the age of 8. Infant teacher training is normally sufficient to enable teachers to 'teach' art to the 0–7 age range. At about 8, the child ceases to produce art work in a spontaneous way. He becomes more critical, more self-critical. After 8 years his question is likely to be not 'May I paint?' but 'How do I paint?' At this stage he will need visual vocabularies to express his ideas. He will need basic skills to translate and transcribe his experiences. The child who cannot write or spell, and does not know the meaning of words, cannot produce creative writing. He needs the basic skills of handwriting, spelling and vocabulary to express himself in a literary or verbal way. All teachers possess the basic language skills and it is reasonable to suppose they can make them available to the children; but those same teachers too frequently do not possess the basic skills of art. Their schooling and, later, training in college did not necessarily, except in a small proportion of their numbers, provide them with the basic art skills. They will not, therefore, be able to pass on any art skills to the children; yet 99·9 per cent of junior school teachers are required to 'teach art'. The dire result of this anomaly is all too plain to see in junior schools, especially in the work of the children of 9, 10 and 11 years. The plain fact is that a large proportion of '8 plus' children, who have reached a stage of development when they need teachers with at least some specialist knowledge, are being taught by teachers who, through no fault of their own, have inadequate training, and in some cases (i.e. teachers of the older generation), no training at all in art.

This problem, which is not peculiar to art, is one which ultimately will have to be solved by radical modification of staffing in schools and re-orientation of courses in colleges of education and teacher training.

In addition, colleges of education will need to construct new courses of a practical pedagogical nature aimed at providing student teachers with a grounding in the elements of art and the basic skills of art and so with insight and understanding of the significant and specific value of arts and crafts as education, and of the unique experiences they provide which cannot be obtained from any other source. The current practice of providing experience in teaching art by sessions of 'curriculum art' is not enough. The relationship between education departments and art departments (and, of course, other specialist departments), in colleges of education should be re-examined. Situations have been observed where art for the personal development of the student is deemed to be the business of the college of education art department, and on the other hand method and content of teaching art in infant/junior classrooms are seen to be the business of the education departments. Where such dichotomy exists it is likely that outmoded 'junior art' clichés will persist, with deleterious effects upon the pupils. There is room for much closer co-operation between teachers in schools and staff in colleges dealing with teacher training. Let the teachers in the schools be invited to talk to student teachers about particular aspects of their work. Let colleges and schools share and exchange ideas, exhibitions of work, books, materials.

Pedagogical thinking should be in terms of education *through* art, not education *in* art. Colleges should 'work towards helping the student to acquire an understanding of the organisation of art learning-situations, to coming to terms with the logic of the subject, the logic of the child, and the logic of the child face to face with his subject,' to quote Professor Ross of Lancaster University.

Perhaps most of all it is necessary to rethink 'what are the basic essential art and craft skills', and how far these should be taught to teachers and to pupils.

The fact must be faced that at the moment the training of junior school teachers to teach art, and the teaching of art and craft to the 8–11 age range in schools, is, in a majority of cases, unsatisfactory. Future policy should call for studies in depth, with research and experiment, of:

1. The possibilities of team-teaching, with special reference to making more art specialist knowledge available in junior schools.
2. Integrated and divergent teaching techniques.
3. The dangers of imbalance produced by too much insistence on projects and themes and of the mistaken belief that painting and craft work which *occur incidentally* during project work are a solution of the non-specialist teacher's art teaching difficulties.

In-service training

Every teacher knows that initial training is only a beginning to the life-long process of acquiring a secure and effective teaching technique and a background of appropriate experience to support it. 'In-service' training provides a means for the teacher to develop continuously his teaching skills and also his professional competence. But running parallel to this need for additional professional training, and complementary to it, is the even greater need—of which we all as teachers are aware—for constant renewal of our lives as people, and for deepening our understanding of the world in which we live.

In the sphere of in-service training the situation is confused. Government education departments, and education authorities, are aware of the need for 'refresher' courses and supplementary training. They provide programmes of courses to meet the need; but, in the schools there are many factors which inhibit teachers from applying for secondment or leave to attend such courses; loyalty to the school, to the head teacher, to colleagues, to the children, are amongst them. Teacher shortage is another cause. Few teachers would enrol for a course if by doing so they know they would impose excessive duties upon their colleagues. On the other hand the teacher who never 'recharges his batteries' during his career will be short of potential before he reaches retirement age, and the children will suffer.

Permission to attend courses is too frequently looked upon as a privilege, a favour or a reward, and the course as a paid holiday. In a democracy which has its educational and financial priorities right it should be written into the professional codes that all teachers should be encouraged, and entitled to attend courses. Every head teacher knows that his children will benefit from having a better-informed and better-equipped teacher. Every education authority knows that money spent on sabbatical leave, non-residential and residential teachers' centres, courses, lectures and above all on supply staff to replace teachers undergoing in-service training, is money well spent.

Money must, eventually, be made available for all serving teachers, as of right, to take sabbatical leave at least every seven years on full pay, if they so wish. Exchange of teachers between countries should be made easier; and why not extend this to teacher exchanges between towns, between schools?

Self-training

In the end, however, no matter how fully his authority provides for his in-service training, however enlightened, encouraging and accommodating his head teacher, it is the teacher himself who can do most to enrich his own teaching repertoire both professionally and personally by taking thought, by reading, by looking at the appropriate TV series, by visiting the pertinent museums, exhibitions, theatres, concerts, lectures. Various courses in art and craft subjects are provided in evening institutes; skills acquired there can be translated into appropriate material for the 'upper junior'. I recall the fascinating and exquisite work in jewellery in non-precious materials produced by one group of children whose teacher joined an evening jewellery class. But above all, the teacher can help himself most by deliberately and thoughtfully training his own perceptions, visual, tactile, auditory, olfactory. The viewfinder exercise (page 51) would benefit the teacher every bit as much as the pupil. Discovery can be as new, as real and as exciting for the adult as for the child.

Re-appraisal of the content of courses for the training of general teachers who will be required to teach art in junior schools and of the understanding of, and provision for, art for the 'upper junior' pupils is long overdue. Art in the junior school has been impotent for too long. Today there are signs of drift. The cure must be sought in reforming junior school art teaching in a new educational mould. Until this hoped-for day we who teach the 8-, 9-, 10-, 11-year-old children can but work out our own salvation. To do so we must make the maximum use of all available opportunities, we must develop our own interests and sensitivities and sharpen our own awareness of the world around us.

If we do this, then, in the interim period, we shall be offering to the pupils the best of which we are capable.

Part Two

Basic skills

The child's sojourn in the junior (7–11) school is a time for, amongst other things, acquiring the essential basic skills which will equip him to engage successfully in the more sophisticated learning activities at secondary level. In these final pages, a number of creative skills are outlined and materials for carrying them out are suggested. The potential of each for providing situations in which the children can become involved in creative experience of the elements of art is stated. Book titles are quoted for those teachers who may feel drawn to study any of the skills or media in greater detail.

The aims of this section are: simple explanation, implantation of ideas, and to provide an indication of the sort of art and craft media and techniques one would hope to see in the junior school; to give some idea of what is involved in organisation and practical knowledge required.

All of the activities described can be carried out in the junior classroom. The teacher need not be an art specialist.

Composition

Drawing and painting have been dealt with earlier in the book but the question of 'composition', which affects both, and indeed any other form of art work, has not been mentioned as such. The 11-year-old is quite capable of making assessments of the more obvious aspects of graphic composition.

One, perhaps the most basic, aspect of composition, in painting and drawing, is the dividing up of the main shape, the paper or board, into subsidiary shapes. Try the following experiment. Take a rectangle or square piece of paper. Ask the pupils how many shapes it represents. The answer should be 'one'. Draw a line across it, as in fig. 86a, and ask the same question again. This time the answer should be three. Put a short line in the larger rectangle (see fig. 86b) and ask the question again. This time there will be some doubt. The most obvious answer is there are three shapes and

fig. 86

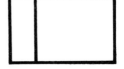  

a   b   c

two of them have a line inside. Now, if you join the short line to the outline as in fig. 86c, the answer to 'how many shapes' will be 'at least six'.

The division of the paper, or board, or lino, or whatever is being used to work on, is an important part of any kind of graphic work. Pupils show great interest in this phenomenon, and they almost always show surprising sensitivity to it. Try other permutations of shapes and lines, and joinings of lines. Show them an appropriate painting by Ben Nicholson or Piet Mondrian.

Balance is a subtler concept but the junior child can begin to comprehend it. They react instinctively to the following test:

Make two clear line drawings big enough to be seen from a distance by every child taking part (see figs. 87a, b) and ask which one is balanced.

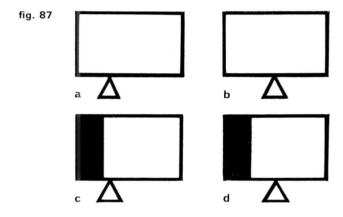

fig. 87

Make another pair (figs. 87c, d) and ask the same question. Then look with the children at their own paintings, with the above balance concept in everybody's mind and see whether it can be decided if their pictures are balanced.

A third experiment is as follows:

Provide a rectangular piece of paper and a number of assorted smaller square and rectangular shapes of different coloured paper. Ask them to arrange three or four pieces of paper within the larger sheet so that they look balanced. Provide adhesive so that the arrangements may be stuck and so made permanent. Again invoke Ben Nicholson and Piet Mondrian. The teacher will probably be surprised to find that children of 10 and 11 show a high degree of discrimination in this matter of basic aesthetics, providing they are not persuaded to accept the teacher's concepts.

The important point to make is that children should be given the opportunity to encounter these ideas and to experiment. Their reactions may sometimes be unexpected, but once the idea is implanted it will remain and perhaps subconsciously it will have its effect upon their creative thinking. Hitherto, in the main, so called 'picture making' has been the nearest approach to composition in the graphic sense, and this usually consists of urging the child to 'fill the paper'. There is much more to it than that, and much more than is mentioned above; but the simple beginnings suggested are well within the child's competence and will provide a groundwork for future departures.

Printing

Two simple printing techniques are as follows:

fig. 88   Crushed paper print   fig 89   Potato print

Crushed paper print

Use a tin lid with an eighth of an inch of ink in it. Roll a piece of stiff paper into a ball, dip and print.

Notice how block is used to make (1) a pattern, (2) a texture.

Potato print

Prepare an ink pad by putting foam rubber in a tin lid and soak with ink or fluid paint.
(1) Cut a potato in half. Print with it. (2) Cut grooves or holes in the potato to give pattern, and print with it. (3) Cut the other half of the potato into a square. Cut pattern in surface and print. Print (1) with block held the same way each time; to print (2), turn block 90° forward after first print and 90° back after next print, then repeat this for all subsequent prints. Invent other sequences for printing and observe the way the results vary visually, and geometrically. This craft is calculated to stimulate a sense of pattern; discrimination in choice of colour and a sense of craftsmanship. N.B. Ink (paint) can be applied to the block by brush if preferred.

Recommended:

Potato Printing, Susanne Strose, Oak Tree Press, London and Sydney.
Creating with Printing Material, Lothar Kampmann, Van Nostrand Reinhold, New York.

Lino cut

This is a more advanced kind of print-making. Ideally the lino (ordinary thick household linoleum) should be glued to a wood block but many schools dispense with this. A cutting board can be made at almost no cost which makes cutting easier and safer. Fig. 90a shows construction and manner of using.

When the lino block is cut it is inked by using a roller which is first run over an inked slab (fig. 90b) and then over the block (fig. 90c). The paper to receive the print is placed on the inky face and is burnished all over with a hard smooth implement, a spoon handle or with a clean roller. Pull up a corner, check, and reburnish if not covered.

Lino blocks are durable, can be used to print on fabric, and can be used by commercial printers for printing school publications (if made type-high).

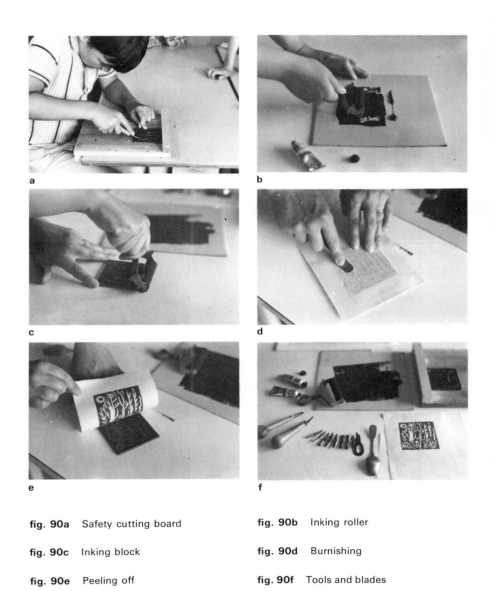

fig. 90a   Safety cutting board   fig. 90b   Inking roller

fig. 90c   Inking block   fig. 90d   Burnishing

fig. 90e   Peeling off   fig. 90f   Tools and blades

Recommended:

Introducing Linocuts, Jane Elam, Batsford, London, and Watson-Guptill, New York.

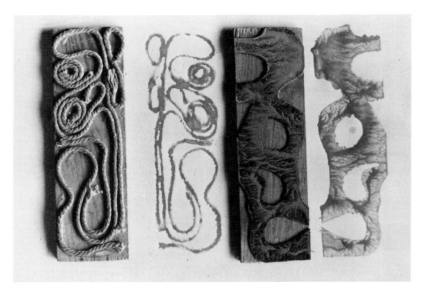

figs. 91 (a) String block (b) String print (c) Card block (d) Card print

String and card block

Two other methods of block printing are: (1) string block, and (2) card block.

The fundamental difference is that the printing surface is produced by sticking it to the block face, not by cutting into the face as in lino or potato. Fig. 91a, b shows a string block and a print made by it. The inking is best done by roller as in the case of the lino block; but ink can be applied with a stiff brush or from a pad as with potato. Fig. 91c, d shows a block produced by sticking a design cut from thick cardboard to the wood block face, and a print made from it. Inking is achieved as above.

Adhesives are important for both these types of block. A waterproof adhesive is necessary such as clear Bostik I. Waterproof adhesive is essential; otherwise the water-based dyes or inks would loosen, and probably detach, the string or card design.

When sticking string or card this should be done under pressure; a pile of books, or a heavy stone or brick; pattern, texture, colour are the elements involved.

Recommended:

Creative Print Making, Peter Green, Batsford, London, Watson-Guptill, New York.
Print making without a Press, J. D. Erickson and A. Sproul, Van Nostrand Reinhold.

Monoprint

An impervious hard working surface is necessary. A formica table is best; a sheet of glass is as good but less safe; Lino ink can be used, or oil paint, or powder colour. Lino ink is probably best. Apply colour to working surface with brush or roller; interesting effects can be achieved by rolling one colour over another. Next draw into the surface with a stick, finger, or brush (fig. 92a) until the desired design is achieved. Place paper over top. Press firmly all over. Peel off.

fig. 92a Drawing into ink

fig. 92b Placing paper on

fig. 92c Print lifted

fig. 92d Second print more highly worked

This is a 'one-off', or at the most 'two-off', technique, and is likely to develop the pupil's linear and textural sense and also quicken the mind to a sense of opportunism and making use of accidental effect.

Screen printing

This fascinating craft can be attempted with very simple means. It is primarily the principle of the stencil. The essentials are a wooden frame over which is stretched a covering of some kind of permeable material, organdie or nylon mesh (old nylon tights are ideal, even if laddered), a squeegee, paper to make the stencil, and colour.

fig. 93a

fig. 93b

fig. 93e

fig. 93f

Fig. 93a b shows a simple wooden frame made from 1 × 1 in soft wood, nailed at the corners, covered with organdie.

Fig. 93c shows the placing of the stencil, or mask, on the paper upon which the print is to go.

Fig. 93d shows the screen placed over it.

Fig. 93e, pouring the colour which is made from ordinary powder colour plus decorator's paste, not too thick, about the consistency of cream.

Fig. 93f shows the squeegee, a piece of hardboard 5 × 2 in, firmly wiping the ink across the whole of the area inside the frame.

Fig. 93g shows the print.

This can now be repeated to give an overall pattern on a long length of paper.

It is best to print on a soft surface. A pad of newspapers will serve, or an old blanket, spread over the table.

This craft compels the pupil to choose and evaluate one shape as against another. It also sets him searching for shape as shape within the environ-

fig. 93c   fig. 93d

fig. 93g

ment in an attempt to find ideas to use as motifs in the printing. The finished prints may be suitable for use in the classroom for decoration of various kinds.

Recommended:

Silk Screen as a Fine Art, Van Nostrand Reinhold, New York.

Introducing Screen Printing, Anthony Kinsey, Batsford, London, and Watson-Guptill, New York.

Simple Screen Printing Techniques, Anthony Kinsey, Society for Education through Art, 29 Great James Street, London, W.C.1.

fig. 94a   Positive rubbing   fig. 94b   Negative rubbing

Rubbings

Rubbing is an extremely simple technique. If a piece of thin paper is placed on an uneven surface and if the paper is then rubbed with a coloured crayon or pencil the texture of the surface beneath will be revealed (see fig. 94a). If a white paper is rubbed over with a colourless wax candle and a wash of colour painted over the rubbed portion, the rubbing will remain white and the texture of the surface will be revealed as a result of the colour being unable to penetrate the wax and consequently only tinting the background (fig. 94b). By these two methods one achieves a positive effect (1) and a negative effect (2). The second has a touch of magic about it which children greatly enjoy.

Because this medium is so expressive it has particular aesthetic and educational value. It provides immediate and direct experience of texture. It is an effective way to induce visual exploration. 'See how many "line textures" you can find; how many "knobbly" textures; how many "man-made" textures,' and so on. Make a scrap book of rubbed textures. Make a set of six-inch modules and assemble them all together to form a large-scale decorative panel, each child providing one module.

The basic printing skills described above are presented singly, but readers will realise the possibility of combining one or more, or all of these, to produce highly intricate and involved works by either single pupils or groups working together. It is probably in this kind of work that the 9-, 10-, 11-year-old achieves his most intense creative fervour. He feels able to 'do' these things. He is not inhibited by not being able to 'draw so that it looks right'.

If you rub a rough, old wall, it can't be wrong.

The inducement to search the environment is self-evident, and it is an extremely flexible activity, which cannot but result in the children becoming more aware of the textural aspects of their environment.

Recommended:

Creative Rubbings, by Laye Andrew, Batsford, London, Watson-Guptill, New York.
Rubbings and Textures, J. J. Bodo, Van Nostrand Reinhold, New York.

Clay skills

In this age of 'plastics' clay for schools is delivered, ready for use, in polythene bags. It is moist and malleable and in perfect condition. Administratively this is convenient, but educationally a good deal is lost. For pottery to be totally creative the potter—child or adult—must experience the excitement of digging and preparing his own clay. This fascinating process is dealt with by Seonid Robertson in *Beginning at the Beginning with Clay*.

Let us, however, assume that clay is available. Once the bag is opened the clay will begin to dry out. For storing re-tie the neck of the bag and, for good measure, store in metal bins. Clay which has dried out completely, so long as it has not been fired, can be reconstituted by breaking it up into small pieces (sugar-lump size if you can spare the time), putting it into a bucket and pouring water over it. A little practice will show how much. If you put too little water it will be totally absorbed. If too much it will remain unabsorbed after twenty-four hours. When the clay has softened take out a handful. It is an easy matter to homogenise it by kneading it, and by rolling and bending it.

Do not waste clay; cost of carriage makes bought clay quite an expensive material.

Coil and thumb pots

Take a piece of clay and roll it out into a long thin sausage. Next coil a base (fig. 95). Make more coils and join to the outside edge of the base. Build upwards and, as you do, join the coils together by scraping-over the joins between. Continue until you reach the height you require.

fig. 95

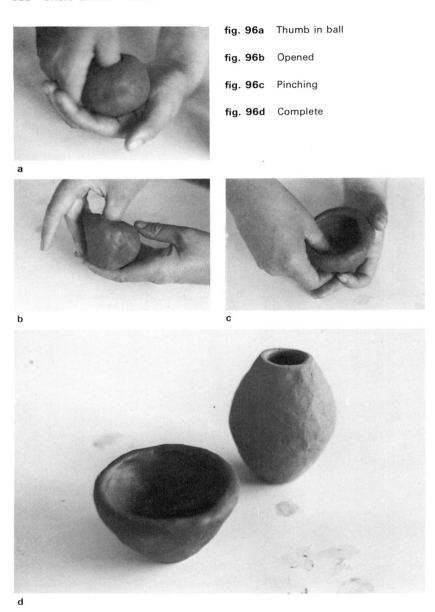

fig. 96a   Thumb in ball

fig. 96b   Opened

fig. 96c   Pinching

fig. 96d   Complete

a

b   c

d

Fig. 96d, above, is the simplest form of pot. It is called a 'thumb' or 'pinch' pot. It is produced by taking a piece of clay and making it into a sphere. Push the thumb through the centre until it is within half an inch of the far side. Then, with the thumb kept in that position, gradually turn the ball round, half an inch at a time, pinching thumb and forefinger together each time. The interior hole will get bigger and the pot will take shape. With perseverance and care beautiful pots can be made by this method. The large pot in fig. 96d is made by inverting one pinch pot on top of another and by smoothing the join and opening a hole in the bottom/top.

fig. 97a Piece of clay being cut

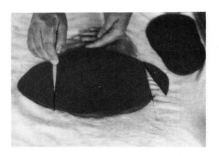

fig. 97b Scratches and joining

fig. 97c Box and incomplete
cylinder

Slab pots

With a rolling-pin or other wooden roller roll out a flat slab of clay. Cut it
into pieces of appropriate size for what you want to make (fig. 97a). Take
some slip (clay mixed with water until it is liquid cream consistency),
scratch the edges (fig. 97b) you want to join, and add a layer of slip, to act
as cement. Press edges together. Continue till box is complete.

Fig. 97c shows a cylinder made by bending one large slice of clay round
until the opposite ends can be joined.

fig. 97d Ceramic panel

fig. 97e Pew group

Fig. 97d shows a Nativity panel (relief) made from modelled clay slab tiles.

Fig. 97e shows a figure made from slabs by a 9-year-old girl.

Modelling

The bus queue illustrated in fig. 98a is a group work made by twenty 11-year-old boys in one afternoon. Each boy made one figure. One boy made the slab base and one boy made the dog. The figures were made by the simple device of rolling out different sized sausages and joining them with slip. They then joined on belts, scarves, hats, etc. and finally joined the figures to the base and to each other to form a queue. The result miraculously survived the drying process and the firing.

Clay work is a three-dimensional craft which provides unique tactile experiences as well as introducing the pupils to concepts of form.

fig. 98a Bus queue

fig. 98b Clay beads, biscuit and glazed, by 11-year-old boys and girls

Recommended:

Beginning at the Beginning with Clay, Seonid Robertson, pamphlet, available from Society for Education through Art, 29 Great James Street, London, W.C.1.

Simple Pottery, Kenneth Drake, Studio Vista, London, 1966, Watson-Guptill, New York.

A Potter's Book, Bernard Leech, Faber & Faber, London.

Handbuilt Pottery, Mollie Winterburn, Mills & Boon, London, 1966.

Making Pottery without a Wheel, F. C. Ball, Van Nostrand Reinhold, New York.

Creative Clay Design, E. Rottger, Van Nostrand Reinhold, New York.

fig. 99a   fig. 99b

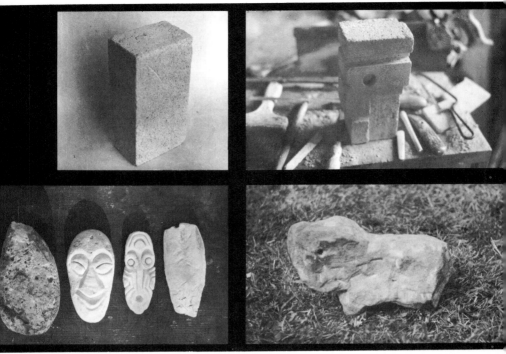

fig. 99c   fig. 99d

Carving

Children enjoy cutting, hacking and rasping at solid blocks of material until they finally achieve a sculptured form of some kind. Wood, polystyrene, plaster, blocks of soap, and blocks such as breeze blocks, Thermalite, Durox, and soft bricks such as those from Derbyshire Silica Brickwork Co. Ltd, Friden, Hartington, nr. Buxton, are all suitable.

Ordinary builder's plaster can be made into convenient-sized blocks by mixing with water and pouring it into cardboard cartons of various sizes.

The illustrations above are:

Fig. 99a, a soft building brick before carving.

Fig. 99b, the same brick carved.

Fig. 99c, carving of a seashore chalk pebble and a carving made from a cuttle-fish bone (obtainable from pet shops or the seashore).

Fig. 99d shows a piece of garden rockery stone on which a determined boy of 8 years spent the best part of a summer holiday with his father's stone-carving chisels and a hammer to produce what he called 'a lion'. The resulting product is not very relevant. The tussle the boy had with the material was significant; as was his determination and application to the job in hand.

Recommended:

Starting with Sculpture, Robert Dawson, Studio Vista, London, and Watson-Guptill, New York.
Building with Balsa Wood, John Lidstone, Van Nostrand Reinhold, New York.
Creative Wood Design, Ernest Rottgen, Van Nostrand Reinhold, New York.

Puppetry

Puppetry is one of the most creative of crafts. It provides close links between craftwork (making puppets), painting (scenery), handicraft (making theatres and apparatus), creative writing (of plays), speech training, music, drama, and the benefits of team working.

Shadow puppets, glove puppets, rod puppets and string puppets (marionettes) all have their devotees, and each variety has its particular characteristic.

fig. 100a   **fig. 100b**

fig. 100c   **fig. 100d**

Shadow puppets

Figs. 100a, b, c, d are supported by rods, with articulated arms, legs, and heads operated also by rods. They are held against the back of a translucent screen, in such a way that their shadow is cast on to the back of the screen. They have the advantage that they are simple to make, require no painting and can be cut out of almost any material . . . it does not matter if 'corn flakes' is printed all over them. The shadow silhouette looks the same. It is the two-dimensional shape which matters. Fig. 100a shows wire puppets covered with coloured cellophane; these produce a coloured shadow on the screen. The images in fig. 100c are made by nailing offcuts of wood to make 'fish' shapes.

fig. 100e   Glove puppets

Glove puppets

Glove puppets are almost equally simple, and most junior children can sew
sufficiently well to make the gloves. Tennis balls, ping-pong balls, old
stuffed stockings, papier-mâché can be used to make heads. They are
colourful when painted and easy to dress and manipulate (fig. 100e).

Rod and string puppets

Rod puppets can be two-dimensional or three-dimensional, can be made
from cloth, paper or almost any material. They are easier to manipulate
than string marionettes, and results can be achieved quickly.

It might be thought that string marionettes are too intricate to make and
too difficult to manipulate for them to be popular in junior school. This is
not true, but it might be wise to experiment with the simpler forms of
shadow and glove puppets first before embarking upon projects involving
marionettes. See book list below.

Remember 'the play is the thing!' To make puppets and not to perform a
play is like planting a farm and never harvesting it.

Recommended:

Puppetry Today, Helen Binyon, Studio Vista, London, 1966, and Watson-Guptill, New
   York.
Introducing Puppetry, Peter Frazer, Batsford, London, 1968, and Watson-Guptill, New
   York.
Presenting Marionettes, Susan French, Van Nostrand Reinhold, New York, 1964.
Simple Puppetry, Sheila Jackson, Studio Vista, London, 1969, Watson-Guptill, New York.

Fabric

The fabric skills include appliqué, embroidery, batik, tie and dye, and screen and block printing. All can be practised in their simple forms in the junior school. Where conditions are propitious these skills can be carried to a high level. One recalls the children who visited Kelmscott Manor, home of the nineteenth-century British designer, William Morris, and followed up by making a study of his fabrics and wallpapers. They made cuttings and printed reproductions of blocks, and, finally, their own fabric printing blocks 'in the manner of' William Morris, with social history as a lively part of the project.

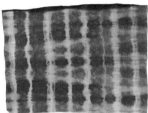

fig. 101a Tie/dye stripes

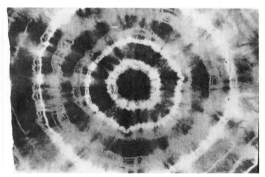

fig. 101d Tie/dye rings

fig. 101b, c

Tie and dye

The principle in tie and dye is that the tie acts as a constriction tight enough to prevent the dye penetrating into the cloth. Figs. 101b and c show two pieces of cloth tied with string.

Figs. 101a and d above show simple examples of tie and dye. In the case of figs. 101c and d a stone was tied into the cloth. Cloth and stone were then dipped into a bowl of dye, and then hung up to dry. When untied they revealed the resulting design (fig. 101d). Each child in the class tied and dyed a square the same size. These were ironed and finally stitched together to make a large wall-hanging. One or two others made cushion covers. The other tie, a simple roll of cloth, produces stripes (figs. 101a and b).

Other methods of tying cloth result in differing patterns.

Recommended:

Tie and Dye, Anne Maile, Mills & Boon, London, 1965.

fig. 102   Appliqué, needlework and embroidery

Appliqué, fabric collage and embroidery

Appliqué, fabric collage and embroidery have a natural affinity and can play their part individually or in combination. One occasionally sees all the above employed together and used in conjunction with block and screen printing and batik. The possibilities within such combinations are limitless, and it is not necessarily a girls' subject or exclusively the field of the women teachers.

Work of this kind provides opportunity to explore colours, textures of materials; to select, to try out, to reject. Collage and appliqué put the child in the position of making aesthetic choices from available materials with differing characteristics.

Recommended:

Design in Fabric and Thread, Aileen Murray, Studio Vista, London, 1969, and Watson-Guptill, New York.
Creative Textile Design and *More Creative Textile Design* by Rolf Hartung, Van Nostrand Reinhold, New York.
Stitchery, H. Krevitsky, Van Nostrand Reinhold, New York.

Batik

Batik, a method of dyeing patterns into cloth, is becoming more and more popular as an art medium, and schools are among the enthusiasts.

It is basically a wax-resist principle. A design is applied to cloth, with clear melted wax, using the traditional tjanting, shown in fig. 103, or alternatively a brush. When the wax cools and hardens the cloth is immersed in dye. Where the wax is, the dye cannot go. The cloth is removed from the dye and is dried. The wax is then removed either by ironing between absorbent paper or blotting-paper, with a hot iron, or by boiling, or by scraping off.

Batik can be carried out on paper but the ironing process must be used to remove wax—it is not practicable to immerse paper in boiling water! With

fig. 103 Batiks and tjanting

children there is a safety factor to consider with this process. The characteristic quality of batik is the crackle effect produced when dye penetrates the cracks which occur in the wax covering.

Batik is a subtle art calling for thought and careful pre-planning, especially when one colour is dyed over another.

Recommended:

Introducing Batik, Evelyn Samuel, Batsford, London, and Watson-Guptill, New York.
Batik for Beginners, Norma Jameson, Studio Vista, London, Watson-Guptill, New York.
Batik, N. Krevitsky, Van Nostrand Reinhold, New York.

Fabric printing

A beginning can be made quite simply in this important craft area by printing with potato blocks on inexpensive cotton material. Helizarin and Tinolite dyes should be used, and these can then be made fast by the simple process of ironing with a hot iron. There is nothing quite so exciting for the girls as to invent a design, print it on cloth, and then to appear at school in a skirt or dress made from their own fabric.

After first experiments with potato, other blocks may be tried (see pages 114, 116.

The designs on the girls skirt-lengths, and made-up skirts, in the illustration below were produced with lino blocks.

fig. 104 Junior girls in skirts made of own material

Recommended:

Introducing Textile Printing, Nora Proud, Batsford, London, 1968, Watson-Guptill, New York.
Simple Print Making, Cyril Kent and Mary Cooper, Studio Vista, London, and Watson-Guptill, New York.
Design on Fabrics, M. P. Johnston and G. Karfman, Van Nostrand Reinhold, New York.

fig. 105 Stone, coal, etc., mosaic head

Mosaic

The principle of mosaic is that the picture is gradually built up from individual and more or less uniform pieces of material, or tesserae, set into or on to a background. The peak of mosaic as an art form was achieved in

Italy at Ravenna in the fourth century and later in Venice in the thirteenth century.

The basic principle can be explored by making coloured tesserae from paper, wood, lino; by using seeds, bottle-tops, etc. Fig. 106 was made by two 10-year-old boys from offcuts of felt left over from the making of soft toys. But the genuine mosaic effect, and experience, can only be achieved by using stone, glass or ceramic tesserae set in plaster or cement.

fig. 106 Felt mosaic

Small pebbles can be collected. It is especially easy and rewarding to do this on the beach. One party is set to collect black pebbles, another white, another intermediate tones or colours. Gravel pits can be equally productive. For town schools tesserae can be made by chipping bricks (red), coal (black), broken pottery (white). I recall a plentiful supply of white produced by breaking up an old marble wash-stand top. One can make miniature mosaics by using broken egg-shells. Coloured glass can be used. Roads and roadworks often use granite chippings of varying colours.

Fig. 105 was made from brick, stones, coal and white granite chips. The container was made from hardboard and wood strips. This was then filled with slow-drying plaster retained by three or four nails set in the base before the plaster was poured in. The 'tesserae' were then set in and the plaster was allowed to set.

Scouring the district for materials for tesserae and, when tesserae were assembled, choosing the colours; creating the textures of the head, the visual and tactile excitement of assembling the work, all provided significant educational experiences of colour, texture, pattern and shape. The pebble collecting especially provided subtle experience of judging colour. The children discovered that pebbles look dull when dry, and were thrilled to see the colours return when the pebbles were immersed in shallow trays of water in the classroom.

It is possible to polish beach pebbles to a gem-like finish. To do this you need an electrically driven 'tumbler'. It consists of a revolving barrel. The pebbles are put inside and the barrel is revolved continuously for a number of days. Tumblers are modestly priced, the smallest being about £5. They can be obtained from M. L. Bleach Products, Ltd, 41 Church Street, Twickenham, Middlesex, England.

Recommended:

Making Mosaics, John Berry, Studio Vista, London, Watson-Guptill, New York.

Paper

When considering what kind of art and craft activities to make available to the junior child, traditionally one tends to think of painting, drawing, printing, modelling and so on.

It provides a new angle, if, instead, one thinks in terms of materials rather than media. For instance, Paper, Wood, Wire, String, Cane, Metal . . . Let's take the first of these and ask the questions: 'What do we use paper for?' . . . 'What could we use paper for?'

Paper is a basic essential of most art activities. It is also unusually useful as a medium. One thinks of papier-mâché, in its various forms, for making puppet heads, masks, animals, models, etc.; laminated skins of glued or pasted paper laid over wire netting to make large structures.

Japanese origami, paper sculpture, Polish paper-cuts, decorations for festive occasions, all evoke specific images. Fig. 107 is typical of the Michael Grater series of books on paper skills. See list at the end of this section. Fig. 108a shows a relief made from modules of cut paper patterns. We are all familiar with the stage artist who tears patterns from newspaper; children enjoy doing this. Fig. 108b is a collage owl made from torn newspaper. Fig. 108c is a paper collage of images, taken from journals of

fig. 107   Paper sculpture   **fig. 108b**   Collage owl

various kinds, which produce a picture relating to 'Pop' art. Fig. 108d is a cut paper collage.

The structure in fig. 108e is built from newspaper. Take a sheet of newspaper and roll it, starting from one corner (fig. 108e), secure it with a dab of adhesive, so that the roll does not spring open; when enough rolls are available building can begin. Joints are made by cutting a 'V' shape at the end of the roll. This produces a snug fit. Add a blob of adhesive at the joint and secure with a dressmaker's pin until the adhesive has set. Building in this way involves the children in direct experience of mathematics, three-dimensional concepts, pattern and design; and the construction will not stand unless the problem of balance is solved in a practical way.

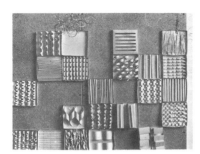

fig. 108a Relief of paper-cuts

fig. 108c Magazine collage

fig. 108e Making newspaper rolls and structure

fig. 108d Paper collage

Recommended:

Creating with Coloured Paper, Lothar Kampmann, Batsford, London; Van Nostrand Reinhold, New York.

Make it in Paper, Michael Grater, Mills & Boon, London.

Paper Faces, Michael Grater, Mills & Boon, London.

One Piece of Paper, Michael Grater, Mills & Boon, London.

Paper People, Michael Grater, Mills & Boon, London.

Creative Paper Design, Ernst Rottger, Van Nostrand Reinhold, New York.

The Dryad catalogue lists a total of seven titles on paper crafts, mostly very modest in price.

Wood

The figures on this page show varied ideas which evolve from wood.

Fig. 109a shows variations on the theme of ships; produced by a lad of 8 years given free use of adult woodworking tools.

The balsa wood carving in fig. 109b is more conventional and made from material provided by the school.

A structure (fig. 109c) built with balsa and other strips of wood.

fig. 109a   Wood ships

fig. 109b   Balsa carving   **fig. 109c**   Balsa structure

Recommended:

Building with Balsa Wood, John Lidstone, Van Nostrand Reinhold, New York.
Creative Wood Design, Ernst Rottgen, Van Nostrand Reinhold, New York.

Wire

The use of wire as support for figures in papier-mâché, and in conjunction with plaster of paris, is well known; as is chicken wire used as a basis for large structures.

It can also be used to make wire sculptures as such.

fig. 110a, b Wire and papier-mâché man and woman
Stages 1 and 2

Stages 3 and 4   **fig. 110c**   **fig. 110d**

The primitive rabbit was made by a 7-year-old boy who was very distressed by the sudden death of his pet rabbit. His father had shown him how to use an electric soldering iron. As can be seen, the lad had mastered this difficult skill.

The making of a wire model is equivalent to making a linear definition of a form. The experience could be expected to help the child to grasp a little of the implication of structure.

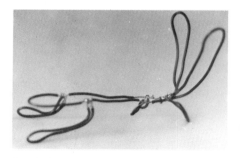

fig. 110e   Peter's rabbit

fig. 110f   Wire leaf

Junk modelling

Vast quantities of redundant materials are discarded every day, all over the world. Many of them can be used again. A good many will be attractive to look at and provocative in form and, as teachers have been quick to realise, will in the right circumstances prompt children into creative activity of various kinds; building, joining, sticking, cutting, bending, manipulating. A child let loose in the presence of a collection like that in fig. 111a and in possession of tools, good adhesives and paint and brushes will very soon become involved with some kind of 'making'.

The boy in fig. 111b is building a railway system with milk straws and egg boxes. Older children will attempt more adventurous projects.

Ideally the ideas should come from the children's reactions to the materials, in the light of current interests. The role of the teacher should be to suggest techniques, not recipes or instructions for the creation of specific artifacts.

fig. 111a   Typical junk

fig. 111b   Junk model railway

Recommended:

Sculpture from Junk, H. Rasmusen and A. Grand, Van Nostrand Reinhold, New York.

String

The illustration in fig. 112a relates to the book quoted below. Strings and fibres generally are not very expensive and in any case large quantities can be acquired as scrap material. Collect a large box of yarns, wool, hemp, sisal, thread, nylon, rope, and provide hardboard, plywood, cardboard, or other suitable support, and adhesive, and see how the children will enjoy sorting out the textures, tones and qualities. See how they will respond to the idea of teasing, coiling, knotting, plaiting, fraying, twisting, kinking, threading, to form patterns and designs, by arranging them and sticking them in place.

fig. 112a   String abstract   **fig. 112b**

Recommended:
Designing with String, Mary Seyd, Batsford, London, 1968, Watson-Guptill, New York.

Conclusion

It is hoped that this book may help the teacher to meet the art and craft needs of the junior school child when he has passed the transition stage between infant spontaneity and the more mature attitude of the junior pupil.

It suggests the sort of work which is appropriate for the child who is at the second of these two levels.

The experienced teacher knows there is no common age at which the change from 'infant' to 'junior' occurs. It may be at 7, it might exceptionally be at 11 years. It could be at any age between these two. A graph would show a sharp peak at about 8 years.

The curricula advocated in this book will be appropriate for a majority of 9-, 10- and 11-year-old children, and not appropriate for others of that age; they will be suitable for a minority of 7-year-old children and not for others. The criterion is one of maturity. The child's chronological age is not very relevant. The realistic factor is his developmental age.

Once the pupil has moved forward from his spontaneous mode of performance as an 'infant', to the questioning and thinking attitude of the 'junior' stage, he is ready to tackle the kind of activities indicated in this book.

Further reading

Creative and Mental Growth, Viktor Lowenfeld and Lambert Brittain. Collier-Macmillan, London.
The Macmillan Company, New York. 1964.

Education Through Art, Herbert Read. Faber, London.

Art for Teachers of Children, Chandler Montgomery, Merrill, Ohio. Prentice-Hall International, London.

Art and the Child, Marion Richardson. University of London Press, 1945.

An Experiment in Education, Sybil Marshall. Cambridge University Press, 1963.

Children and Their Primary Schools (2 volumes, 25/- ea.). Her Majesty's Stationery Office, London.

Alongside the Child in the Primary School, Leonard Marsh. A. C. Black Ltd, London, 1970.

European Painting and Sculpture, Eric Newton. Penguin Books, London.

The Meaning of Art, Herbert Read. Faber & Faber, London.

New Horizons in Psychology, edited by Brian Foss. Penguin Books, London, 1966.

Creative Themes, Henry Pluckrose. Evans Bros., London, 1969.

Pictures with Crayons
Pictures with Inks   Lothar Kampmann. Batsford, London, 1968.
Pictures with Paints

Taking Casts in Sand, Roy Bell. Pergamon Press, London, 1970.

Creative Crafts for Today, John Porchmouth. Ginn & Co. Ltd, London, Studio Vista, London, 1969.

Looking and Seeing Books 1, 2, 3, 4, Kurt Rowland. Reinhold.

Learning to See Books 1, 2, 3, Kurt Rowland. Reinhold.

Index

Action painters 102
Ammonite 95
Art appreciation 43, 102
Art specialist teachers 98
Art teacher/non-art teacher 73

Backwardness 88
Basic skills 76
Batik 131
Beach 37
Beethoven 73, 102
Betjeman, John (Sir) 83
Brushes 29
Butterflies 37

Camera 35, 90
Carving 126
Cave painters 102
Cellophanes 17
Centre of interest 69
Cézanne 55, 67, 107
Chagall 106
Choral symphony 103
Clegg, Sir Alec 97
Coco the clown 79
Collage 13, 57, 61
College of education 109
Colour
    display 95
    environmental 19
    film 90
    games 14
    identification 17
    matching 15
Comparative grades 6
Composition 57, 68, 112
Concorde 80, 82
Creativity 73
Creative writing 65, 66, 83, 106, 108
Crimping irons 95
Crystal garden 95
Cubist painters 75
Curriculum art 109
Curriculum research 97

Display 94
Drawing 40, 46
Drawing media 41
Dressing-up 22, 77

Education through art 109
Egg-timer 95
Environment 62, 67, 83, 90, 92, 120
    classroom 94
    school 90, 96

Equipment 100
Expression 87

Fabric dyes 132
Fabric skills 130
Film, *Seeing Colour* 19
Folk art 37, 63
Form 38
Frazer, Douglas 63

Glass eye 95
Glass prism 15, 95
Goldsmiths College, London 97
Gourd 95
Growth rhythms 61

Hemingway, Ernest 73
Hepworth, Barbara 39
History/art link 44
Hopkins, Gerard Manley 83
Horniman Museum, London 63

Impressionists 102
Indian folk art 63
Indoor plants 95
Inland waterways 69
Integration 8, 68
Interior design 19

Japan, school art 92
Junk 38
Junk modelling 139

Kaleidoscope Orissa 63
Keats 73

Laurie, A. P. 23
Leading questions 86
Leonardo da Vinci 102
Lexicon 14
Light meter 90
Line as line 40
Lipchitz, Jacques 39
Lipton, Seymour 39
Loan services, art 103

Machinery display 95
Mandoline 95
Marvin Medium 24
Mass media 103
Materials 100
Matisse 73
Microscope 91
Modelling, clay 124, 125
Modules 32

Mondrian, Piet 113
Moore, Henry 39
Mosaic 133
Mounts 95
Muller (grinder) 23
Multipurpose areas 68

Natural history/art link 43
New Horizons in Psychology 73
Newspaper, use of 25
Nicholson, Ben 113

Oil pastel 25
Open plan 68, 100
Optical mixing 19
Optics 23, 90

Paints
    acrylic 24
    powder 24
    PVA 24
Palettes 29
Papers 25
Paper crafts 136
Pastels 25
Patronage of the arts 103
Pattern
    animal 36
    architectural 36
    repeating 36, 37
Pebbles 36
Pens
    ball-point 41
    bamboo 44
    felt 44
    felt-tipped 41
    fibre-tipped 41
    reed 42
    stick 44
Pestle and mortar 23
Picasso 21, 63, 75
Playgroups 6
Plowden Committee (U.K.) 68
Poster colours 25
Pots
    coil 121
    slab 123
    thumb 122
Prints
    card 116
    crushed paper 114
    lino 115
    monoprint 117
    potato 114
    screen 118, 119
    string 116

Problem-solving 12, 67, 101
Projects 69
starting-points 70
Projector 68, 91
Props 22
Puppetry 68
Puppets
glove 128
rod 128
shadow 127
string 128
PVA binders 25

Radiometer 95
Ravenna 134
Read, Herbert 14
Reading age 89
Renaissance 102
Rock crystal 95
Rousseau, Douanier 102
Rubbings 30, 120
Ruisdael, Jacob 107

School library 102
School visits 105
Schools Council (U.K.) 97
Sculpture
Nigerian 63
paper 135
Sea-horse 95
Sea-urchin 95
Sensitivity 94, 101
to colour 10

Shape 45, 61
Silhouette 45
Sisley, Alfred 107
Slides 91
non-photographic 18
Society for Education
through Art 104
Spectrum 15, 23
Spelling bee 14
Spinning tops 19
Squaring 52, 53
Staple-gun 20, 95
Stein, Gertrude 63
Stethoscope 95
Stimuli 73, 95
Stimulus
dramatic 84
from materials 87
through change 87
verbal 85
visual 77
Stoke Bruerne 69
Stop-watch 95
Storage 95
String 140
Structuring 67
Stubbs, George 85

Tate Gallery, London 106, 107
Team-teaching 66, 108, 109
Television 80, 102
Tempera blocks 24

Textures
drawn 30, 31
found 34
in paint 33
made 34
printed 33
Theme 69
Tie and dye 129
Time-tabling 68
Timber 65
Tjanting 131
Tone-scale 16
Town planning 67
Training
initial 108
in-service 109
self-training 110
Traditional design 69
Transplants 64
Tumbler, polisher 134
Turner, J. M. W. 107

University of Lancaster 97

Variation in conditions 100
Van Gogh 42, 92, 102
Vegetable dyes 23
Viewfinder 51, 57, 66, 80
Visual exploration 120
Visual vocabulary 46
Vocabulary 39

Wagner, Richard 107
Wilson, Richard 106
Wire crafts 138, 139
Wood crafts 137